From Obstacles to Political Victory

KEVIN J. NOLAN SR.

First Edition, 2019

Published by Savory Words Publishing
www.savorywords.com

© 2019

ISBN 978-0-9863552-9-5
Printed in the United States of America

Dedication

I dedicate this book to my dear family, including my wife, Linda and my children, Kevin, Jr., Kristi Ann, and Keith. I am extremely blessed to have a wonderful and supportive family who has given me the chance to have full communication access, resulting in so many special moments over the years. I would also like to acknowledge and thank them for their feedback during the process of writing this book. It is my sincere hope that this book will provide insight into my past and the magnificient journey I have been on.

I also want to acknowledge the editing team at Savory Words Publishing, especially Trudy Suggs, for all of their guidance with this book. With their knowledge and feedback, the process of writing this book was much easier. It has been a pleasure to share my story through my eyes.

"Don't let being deaf stop you.
Try it! Go for it!
I'll always respect you,
whether you succeed or fail."

Kevin J. Nolan Sr.

Table of Contents

Prologue

I looked out over the crowd, people cheering and laughing; I was flabbergasted. How in the world did I go from a naive, isolated little boy who struggled to communicate to being the nation's first city council member who was born deaf? What had I gotten myself into? As laughter flowed through the room, I experienced an influx of emotions while on stage, from relief, to excitement, to nervous anticipation.

These thoughts, among a million others, rushed through my head as I took in the scene. Never did I expect the adventures my work would bring me, nor did I ever expect to have such challenges along the way. But one thing was for sure: I was ready.

CHAPTER 1
Born into a World of Uncertainty

Dad holding me with Mom and brother Bruce in 1946 at our first home in Attleboro.

O n October 8, 1945, the New York Times announced that General George Patton Jr. had turned over command of his beloved United States Third Army to Lt. General Lucian K. Truscott in Germany. It was also reported that Emperor Hirohito of Japan knew of the Pearl Harbor plan, but the Harbor had been attacked 12 hours before he signed the prescript declaring war against the United States. Such was the turmoil of the world that I was brought into—only three days after my father had returned from World War II.

My father, Robert "Bob" John Nolan, was a Navy lieutenant who had seen battle on the USS *Belleau Wood* and was very affected by his war memories. My parents made their home in Attleboro, Massachusetts, a town known as the "Jewelry City," because many high schools and colleges order class rings, championship rings, military rings, emblems, and trophies from Attleboro's jewelry companies. My family ended up in Attleboro when my great-grandfather, Thomas F. Nolan, established a general store, the NOLAN-MCCAMBRIDGE General Store on Main Street. He and my great-grandmother, Agnes, had four children, including my grandfather, Frank. Frank owned Saart Bros, a silversmith manufacturing company, in Attleboro, until my father took over in 1955. In the early 1980s, the company was sold to Texas Instruments Company. I remember visiting the factory with much delight, despite my fears of the huge machines there, because many of the employees spoiled me with candies and graham crackers.

My great-grandfather also served as chairman of the Board of Registrars of Voters for twelve years before his death. Although he was a staunch, long-time Democrat, he never let the question of party lines interfere with his duties as registrar, and candidates who sometimes posed intricate questions to the board strongly praised his fairness and understanding of situations. During his long period of failing health, he rallied, and on the busy days during state and local elections, he carried out his duties as registrar with loyalty and determination, frequently making special trips from his home to aid persons desiring to register.

My father, Bob, graduated *cum laude* from the University of Notre Dame with a bachelor's degree in business. He worked for Haskins and Sells, a New York City accounting firm, and then after the war, worked in his father's silversmith business. My mother, Johanna Mary Doherty (we called her Mary), had attended Bryant College in Rhode Island for a year of secretarial courses. She and my father were high school sweethearts, although they attended different high schools. They had my brother, Robert Bruce, in August 1942, and then me in October 1945. Next was Francis Edward "Ward" in 1949, and my sister Maureen in 1952.

Confirming Suspicions

Although I was their second child, Mary and Bob were certainly not prepared for the surprises I would bring. When I was about two or three months old, my parents began to notice how I did not respond to loud noises such as slamming doors, or things falling to the floor. They suspected I had a hearing problem, so they did what most parents do when they think their children might be deaf: they banged pots and pans together behind my back. Sure enough, I didn't react. They were worried because they had

My father, "Bob," and I enjoyed our time at Cape Cod's Harwichport Beach in 1946.

never met or associated with anyone who was deaf, although one of my father's buddies had a deaf son. They and my grandparents were upset; all they could think of was "deaf and dumb." They were full of questions: Would I be able to speak? Would I ever have a job? What would my life be like?

The fact that I seemed to be deaf was a double whammy to Bob, who had returned from World War II only three days before I was born. Bob was scarred by the horrific memory of his men killed in a kamikaze attack, unable to forget the smell of burning flesh. The possibility of his son being deaf just a few months later was another blow to him.

At the age of one year, I was taken to a doctor who advised that my tonsils and adenoids be removed. At the age of three, in the hopes of restoring my hearing (although I never had any in the first place), my adenoids were removed

3

again, and I was given several radium treatments. Nothing worked, of course. Local doctors eventually referred me to the renowned Johns Hopkins Hospital in Baltimore, Maryland, for evaluations that confirmed everyone's suspicions: I was deaf. The doctors recommended that I be enrolled at the Clarke School for the Deaf in Northampton, Massachusetts. I'm not quite sure what else they said to my parents; my parents never really told me much about their experiences, even when I was older and could ask questions. Like many other parents of that time, they were very private about personal matters. Even so, I wish I could ask them the many questions I have about their decision-making process and choices.

When my sister Maureen was two years old, she was tested at Children's Hospital in Boston. The results reported that she had a 60-70 decibel loss in both ears, and so she was fitted with a body hearing aid immediately. I was nine years old at this time, and had been fitted with a body aid at Clarke School for the Deaf. However, my parents decided to have her attend the local school, since she was hard of hearing and apparently able to understand the spoken word without much assistance. This only made us even more distant, in addition to our age difference.

CHAPTER 2
Finding My Footing

Four generations in 1942: Elizabeth "Bessie" (Robinson) Nolan (my grandmother), Robert John Nolan (my father), Johanna Mary (Doherty) Nolan (my mother), Thomas Francis Nolan (my great-grandfather), Mary (Nolan) Washburn (my aunt), Francis "Frank" Edward Nolan (my grandfather), Robert Bruce Nolan (my older brother), Elizabeth "Betty" (Nolan) Gibbs (my aunt), Agnes (McCambridge) Nolan (my great-grandmother).

I was a healthy and jovial child despite my parents' beliefs about deaf people. Like many other parents of deaf children at the time, my mother corresponded with the famed John Tracy Clinic in Los Angeles, California. The clinic sent her free information about raising a deaf child, along with speech lessons, fun activities, and reports. Helen Watrous, a renowned tutor with the Sarah Fuller Foundation in Boston, also tutored me during my toddler years before I went to Clarke. Even with the private tutoring and speech training, pronouncing "Daddy" proved difficult for me, so

Here I am atop, my father's shoulders in 1947.

I took to calling my father "Bob," a practice that continued until the day he passed away.

I was very active and enthusiastic, traits that were evident long before I was sent to Clarke. I was always alert to my home surroundings, even if I didn't always speak up. Among my family members, I was a very quiet and passive individual, because I never really knew what was going on—that, and I never felt accepted. Even so, I was always eager for social experiences, grabbing any chance to partake in group activities. Although these two sides of me seemed contradictory, it was how I was for most of my younger years.

My sense of humor made me a natural storyteller later in life, and an actor with a talent for imitation, not to mention a terrific prankster. One time, my neighbors and I were playing Cowboys and Indians with toy guns, bows, and arrows. I suddenly fell backward, my chest covered in blood as if wounded by an arrow or bullet. The kids were frightened and ran to their parents screaming for help. Their parents ran to me, horrified, and about to call for the ambulance until they noticed the blood was actually ketchup. Needless to say, they weren't amused. But this wouldn't be the last of my pranks.

Another thing I loved to do was go to the store next door to my great-grandparents' former general store. Every Saturday, my granddad, Frank, would take me in his black Oldsmobile 88 (with a Rocket engine, one of the first in town) to the store, an old-fashioned soda fountain, buying me candy bars and comics. I loved the candy so much that I always had a hard time sharing. "All gone! No more!" I'd say if someone asked me for a piece.

The truth is that my granddad was the only member of the family who truly doted upon me. Frank was a big, tall man who was balding and had an Irish face. A jolly guy, he was always impeccably dressed, often wearing a silk smoking jacket. In fact, I don't remember ever seeing Frank without a shirt and tie, not even when he was at home. He smoked cigarettes—but only with a cigarette holder, pulling cigarettes from a beautiful case. He also smoked pipes that created a distinct tobacco smell that I can easily recall even today. He loved big cars, too, such as Lincolns and Cadillacs; he even had a Pierce Arrow at one point. He was very much the proper gentleman, always a man of means and a class act. I still have a clear picture of his jovial face smiling at me.

Every time I came home from Clarke for the holidays, I would make a beeline to my grandparents' house, which was within walking distance from my house. Once I arrived, I'd look for sparkling glass dishes of chocolates that were scattered throughout the house. When my grandparents weren't looking, I'd grab several pieces and put them in my pockets or a paper bag. Even today, I have a fondness for candy that I consider a memorial to my granddad.

In March 1955, my parents drove to Clarke and picked me up. By now, I was nine years old. I was surprised by their arrival; the school normally told me in advance if they were coming. We spent a couple of nights at Hotel Northampton before Bob finally explained that Granddad had passed away and was now in heaven. Bob took me to the window and pointed at the white clouds, indicating that Granddad was now up there. I struggled to understand his words, and was puzzled because I couldn't find Granddad up there. After several tries, I could still barely understand. That night, I tossed and turned in bed trying to figure out why and how Granddad was gone.

As I was about to go home for Easter, my housemother, Poelbe Murphy, gave me a small pot of flowers for my grandmother, whose name was Elizabeth ("Bessie"), but

I called her Nana. As soon as I got home, I walked to my grandparents' house and gave Nana the flowers, saying, "It's for you because Granddad died." Nana burst into uncontrollable tears. I was so frightened and confused that I panicked. I ran home and asked Bob if I had done something wrong. It was the first time I had seen an adult, especially at her age, cry. I hadn't understood until then how much she missed Frank, mainly because of the limited communication I had with my father. Bob immediately went to Nana's house and talked with her, and told me things were okay.

A few months later, Bob asked me to spend the night at Nana's place to keep her company. I agreed, although I was wary after the last time. Upon learning I would sleep in my granddad's large bedroom (in those days, it was common for people to have separate bedrooms), I became anxious, but said nothing as always. As Nana smiled and said good night, I thought of going back home, but didn't want to upset her.

I went into the room, and looked around. "Holy cow!" I thought. Every single item Granddad had owned was still there. I nervously opened the bedroom closet, and immediately wished I hadn't because his silk robes were still hanging in there. It took me a long time to put on my pajamas and then climb into bed. I covered my head with the heavy bedspread, but still found it difficult to sleep.

The next morning, Nana asked me to get something from Granddad's drawer. I nodded, and found a small box in that drawer. Not knowing what it was, I slowly opened it, and gasped. It was Granddad's false teeth. I was so creeped out that I ran home without saying good-bye, and didn't return to visit Nana for several months. Eventually, as I got older, I realized that Nana was still grieving back then. Had my parents been able to communicate with me more, I likely would have understood better. Still, that experience was a formative one for me.

CHAPTER 3
The Clarke Years

This was my first class at Clarke. I am reading a book to my classmates (left to right), Linda Kessler, Gordon Bergan, Betty Hammel, Nancy Kinkead, and Bernard Brown. (Absent: Tom Fields).

In September 1950, my parents had a daunting decision to make: where to send me for my schooling. There were four oral schools in Massachusetts: Horace Mann Public School, Beverly School for the Deaf, Boston School for the Deaf run by the Sisters of St. Joseph, and Clarke School for the Deaf. Despite both Bob and Mary's strong Irish Roman Catholic roots, and the fact that my great-uncle was a priest, they didn't send me to Boston School for the Deaf. Instead they chose to follow my grandfather Frank's recommendation; he had visited Clarke School and thought it the best fit for me. Sending me to Clarke School for the Deaf was a painful decision for my parents, because it meant I would be sent 100 miles west from home at the age of four and half.

My parents drove for more than three hours across the state to Northampton. Mass Pike hadn't been built at that time. We drove up Round Hill Road overlooking the Connecticut River Valley and arrived at the beautiful campus. The campus consisted of a classroom building covered in ivy, three dormitories, a gymnasium, two pre-vocational buildings, the principal's stately house, a boiler plant, and a cottage for teachers-in-training. Pine trees and maple trees covered the picturesque campus, with birds, squirrels, rabbits, and acorns everywhere.

Northampton, Massachusetts

Northampton was a quiet, but substantial, town that had a long history of storied traditions. Founded in 1654, the formerly-named Nontuck was home to notable people throughout history, such as evangelist and reformer Sojourner Truth, author Lydia Marie Child, inventor of the graham cracker Sylvester Graham, and President Calvin Coolidge. In fact, President Coolidge started his political career as a Northampton city councilor for Ward 2 before becoming the mayor. Northampton also had famous visitors such as abolitionist Frederick Douglas, and engineer and scientist Alexander Graham Bell, who taught the teachers and served on the board of Clarke School during the 1870s. The town is also home to Smith College, whose alumni include Julia Child, Nancy Reagan, and Barbara Bush, among others.

Clarke was also where President Coolidge met his wife, Grace Goodhue. The story goes that Grace, a Vermont native, got a job teaching at Clarke, and one day she was watering the flowers when she looked up. Through a window she saw a thin young lawyer who rented a room at Adams House on campus; he was shaving while wearing a hat on his head. She tried not to stare, but she thought it was odd that anyone would shave with a hat on. Calvin Coolidge caught her gaze through the window and instantly fell in love with her. Grace was trained and taught at Clarke for three years, and served on the school board for many years until her death in 1957.

The Clarke Story

Clarke School for the Deaf was an oral school where only speech and lipreading were taught; sign language was explicitly prohibited. The school was named after its principal benefactor, John Clarke, a Northampton city merchant who lost his hearing in later years. The story of Clarke School for the Deaf begins with the state of deaf education during the nineteenth century. Back in the early 1800s, deaf children in Massachusetts were refused admission into public schools, yet there existed no state school or institution for deaf children. Starting in 1817, deaf children were sent to what is now the American School for the Deaf in Hartford, Connecticut, the first deaf school in America.

On June 1, 1867, the Clarke Institution for Deaf-Mutes was established with the assistance of Gardiner Greene Hubbard, a lawyer and the founder of National Geographic. Hubbard had a deaf daughter, Mabel, who lost her hearing from scarlet fever when she was four; Mabel would later marry Alexander Graham Bell. Clarke was a residential school up to eighth grade, and was dedicated to oral language training 24 hours a day. An extremely formal school like many schools of that time, it emphasized family values and expected the best of manners from its students.

My Early Years at Clarke

I remember very little of the time after my parents dropped me off at campus, although I can remember a large room with six beds in Dudley Hall. During my first week in the Lower School, my teacher Marcia Ackley wrote a postcard letting my parents know how much I enjoyed the school. She also said I was full of fun and mischief, but that was what she expected from her years of working with young children. The report from my last year in Lower School in 1955 read:

"Kevin is a very personable little boy with a good mind and a lot of ability but with an insatiable curiosity for knowing about things that are of no importance to him—a trait that detracts from his attractiveness as well as from his ability. He is an excellent lip reader and has good speech. He has good understanding of language and can do a very good work when he puts his mind to it. He loves to socialize with his peers and adults. He is a storyteller. He loves to tease children. He is also a 'worrier.' He is troubled about many things that should be and other people's concern, and he really cannot rest until he is sure that whatever it is bothering him will be properly attended to. His class was the most interesting and bright group in Lower School. The children have great potential and are hard workers. They are very competitive, are very jealous of one another and are never willing to share honors or to take pride in one another's accomplishments."

Life as a Clarke Student

At Clarke, students spent five years in the lower school, four years in the middle school, and then four years in the upper school. Although the school had students leave after the eighth or ninth grade, many of us left at ages much older than the typical eighth grader. In both the Middle and Upper Schools, we had tutorials and classes after school. On weekends, our time was spent with teachers and housemothers in charge of the residence halls. There were no male houseparents at the time, and most of the housemothers were older, either widowers or unmarried. The housemothers would only say, "Brush your teeth. Time to get up. Clean up your room. Don't do that. Make your beds. Get in line. Time to go to school. Time for bed. You are a naughty boy." There was never any constructive communication or learning experiences. This was a common experience of that generation, even at signing schools.

All students had to obey the rules, regardless of if we liked it or not. We were rarely allowed to question or to talk back, and if we did we risked discipline. We were taught to respect teachers, administrators and housemothers at all times. Furthermore, each student was required to perform chores such as

I'm the 5-year-old looking at the photographer. Headphones to help us "hear" are visible behind our chairs.

sweeping the floors, cleaning the bathrooms, making our beds, doing dining tasks, and raising and lowering the American flag in front of school every day.

Life on campus was indeed very proper. We could not wear play clothes to the dining room. On Sundays, we had to wear formal clothes such as jackets and ties and dresses to every meal. Good table manners were expected at all times. Teachers served every meal to the students, teaching us the names of the food we were eating as well as table manners. Even if a student did not like something on the plate, everybody was forced to eat a little of every food on the table. We were also required to bring and read a book at the table so that no time would be wasted if we had nothing to talk about.

Using our hands to communicate, or even gesture, anywhere on or off campus was expressly prohibited. We lived in fear of breaking this rule; otherwise we would be severely disciplined, or even possibly expelled from school. In fact, we sometimes were required to sit on our hands to avoid using our hands. It often looked like a game of charades when watching schoolmates trying to communicate with each other, because they had to keep changing their facial expressions until the other understood their message.

We couldn't even wave at each other to call each other's attention. This resulted in many students staring at each other pointedly until the other noticed, or making weird faces to try and call attention. We also couldn't use our hands for baseball signals, such as saying, "Strike!" or "Ball!" I challenged the staff on this, but they told me I had to follow the rules.

Boys and girls never played together after school. The teachers and housemothers kept us segregated on the playground and in the playrooms. We also sat separated from each other in a room, even during meetings and assemblies. The only times we sat together were in the classroom and dining room. Often the older girls would go upstairs and look out the windows or stand on the balconies and talk with boys who were on the playground using gestures and lipreading. The only time we could touch each other was during dancing class. Naturally, the boys and girls would find times and places to kiss each other in unsupervised rooms or off campus such as at the park or in downtown. Sometimes, they even snuck into each other's bedrooms.

The school only offered one sporting team: basketball. Girls were not allowed to play sports back then, but there was a cheerleading squad. The girls were always enthusiastic about attending the basketball games because they could see and talk with the boys.

Basketball was, of course, a popular activity, and I played for two years. My frustration was that I tended to play well during practices, but not during games. For some reason, I was often reluctant to shoot the basketball. Panic always set in when I played in front of spectators—there were too many eyes! It is also interesting to think back on how we communicated on the court, especially those who couldn't speak very well. I cringe thinking about how we must have looked to other schools, or how we used exaggerated mouth movements! We simply didn't know any different back then.

The school also offered physical education, skating, snow sledding in the back of Hubbard Hall, bowling, volleyball, and Boy Scouts activities. After school, the boys and I took pre-vocational classes such as printing, cabinet making, art, photography, and drafting classes. I hated these courses because I had no motivation or interest in them. The fact that I was not skilled with my hands did not help at all. I'd often work on the same project for a year while the other boys completed several projects, mainly because I preferred to chat with friends rather than work on my project.

Teachers were on duty every other weekend and spent a lot of time entertaining the students. The students who lived nearby went home for the weekends, but they were required to be back by 8:30 on Sunday morning for Bible school classes. Parents who lived farther away were required to bring back their children to the dormitory before 5:00 p.m., or risk their children being disciplined by being sent to their rooms, skipping supper (with bread and milk brought up to their room instead), and evening activities. Why the children were punished instead of the parents, I never understood.

Despite all the restrictions, the school never lacked students; there was a long waiting list for admissions.

In the Classroom

In the classroom, we fitted our own earphones or hearing aids with a control device. The teacher wore her own microphone, which was actually inconvenient because she had to pull or move the long attached cord every time she walked from one student to another. Oftentimes the teacher became irritated having to untangle the cord, which became a show for the class. She wasn't the only frustrated one, though. Many of the students hated wearing the devices because they were uncomfortable and often made whistling noises, especially if wearing glasses like I did. In fact, today I still have a dent in my now-bald head because of the years of wearing the cumbersome earphones!

Even though some struggled, students were required to speak and lipread. This was extremely difficult for some, embarrassing them to the point where their self-esteem was greatly affected. This also spilled over into their writing, which was often heavily marked in red. To avoid the red marks, they used simple vocabulary rather than the vocabulary they really knew. This was also true for their spoken words; they would use simple words all to save face. This falsely implied to hearing people listening to them

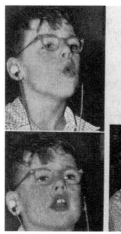

National Geographic featured Clarke School and oral education in its March 1955 issue; here, I am with my classmate Linda Kessler.

that they were simple people with limited vocabularies and language. This, of course, wasn't true; rather, it was a survival method.

Another frustration for the students throughout their years at Clarke was that every time we spoke to a teacher, the teacher would stop us mid-word or mid-sentence to correct our pronunciation. This caused us to lose any interest in pursuing conversations with the teachers, or even forget what we were saying. How this was beneficial to the students' learning continues to be a mystery to me.

The school used the Fitzgerald Key approach to teach language. This was a framework in which visual symbols were used to teach rules for word order. Learning by rote, students often paused to try and remember the rules of English word order; however, rather than actually learning rules, students simply imitated their teacher's spoken language instead of expressing themselves naturally. They were basically parrots repeating what the teacher said until they did it right.

Miss Numbers: A Force to Be Reckoned With

The students especially feared Miss Numbers, the middle school supervising teacher who was a big and heavy white-haired woman. Even the staff feared her, never knowing what to expect from her and her punishment; they secretly called her the "Great White Whale." She was known to bawl out staff in front of the students, or eject teachers-in-training out of the dining room if the table rules weren't followed. Miss Numbers was often seen carrying a candy box, which the students knew held a hairbrush to dole out punishment by hitting their heads, elbows, and hands. I always could feel her evil eyes everywhere, especially at the windows, seeking out every opportunity to punish someone, anyone. It was common to learn that she had opened and read students' personal mail from families; in fact, she often approached me and made fun of my mother's news.

Every time Miss Numbers went to her car, she refused to get inside until a boy opened the car door for her as if she was royalty. Many times the boys would look the other way, pretending they didn't see her waiting for them. Once she got into the car, the car would lean to her side, her weight straining the suspension. The car always seemed to threaten to topple over.

One day, when I was eleven years old, the teacher was upset with my class because we were not paying attention to her. She called Miss Numbers to the classroom. Instead of talking to us as the teacher had requested, Miss Numbers looked around the class with an angry, evil-looking face, and pointed at me, and told me to come up. Like the rest of the class, I was afraid of this woman because of her infamous punishments. I walked, my legs quivering as I tried to figure out what I had done wrong. Again, students couldn't question the reason for any punishment we received. Miss Numbers commanded me to take off my belt and hand it over to her. She then forced me to take my pants down as my classmates looked on in trepidation. She placed me on her lap and whipped my bottom with the belt. After several whips, she got up and left the room without saying a word. To this day, my classmates and I still talk about this horrifying incident of abuse, even remembering that I wore yellow boxer shorts, and wondering what prompted it.

I had one more unforgettable encounter with Miss Numbers. One evening, before supper began, I was asked to bring a meal tray to Miss Numbers' apartment at Gawith Hall, a dorm for middle school students. I knocked on her door, but there was no response. I slowly opened the door and unexpectedly found her sitting on the toilet in the half-bathroom located right next to the front door. Her big fleshy fanny was over hanging the seat. I gasped, but I was too horrified to say anything. I quickly put down her tray on the floor and hightailed it out of there immediately. I feared that I would be severely punished, but nothing ever happened. Maybe Miss Numbers was too embarrassed and did not want to bring it up.

In all truth, Miss Numbers distressed many students at the school. Even today, at reunions or gatherings among Clarke schoolmates, her name always comes up and never with any fondness. She was an abusive teacher who was the epitome of meanness, and she caused deep psychological trauma for many students.

Adventures at Clarke

During the thirteen years I was at Clarke, I blossomed into a jokester who drove everyone up the wall. Even though there were so many rules, I often felt more comfortable interacting with the staff more than the students, especially when conversing about politics and the world. As an excellent lipreader, my peers always made sure I had the seat that gave me the best view of the teachers' table during meals. That way, I could lipread the teachers' conversations and share the contents with my friends. My teachers later admitted that every time they saw me watching them, they felt uneasy because they knew I could easily catch their conversations. In fact, I won Clarke's Best Lipreader award two years in a row.

I fondly remember my years at Clarke because my peers were like brothers and sisters to me, a close family. My class was a bright, competitive group. I had three classmates who I went through school with from the beginning until graduation day: Gordon Bergan, Bernard Brown, and Linda Kessler. Since both Gordon and

Studying microscopic life in pond water in 1962; I'm the second from the left. Note the unplugged headphones some of us are wearing.

Bernard's parents were deaf and also Clarke alumni, I learned a lot from them because they were comfortable with their lives. In their homes with their deaf parents, there was always communication access. Some people ask me how this can be if their parents didn't sign, but because they all were deaf and understood each other, they could converse freely. Today, all four of us choose to use sign language.

Once in a while the boys and I would get restless at school so we'd do things that were considered unacceptable. Gordon especially had the reputation of being energetic and mischievous, always adept at finding something to do that the other boys wouldn't normally do. One day in Rogers Hall, the Upper School dorm, we were curious about a hole in the wall outside near the locker room. Gordon, not knowing where it led to, decided to explore by crawling into the hole, which led to a tunnel. Two others and I followed after him. After some time, we realized we were crawling under Round Hill Road. With my phobia of rats, I began to panic, having no idea of what was ahead in the complete darkness. I began to worry that Round Hill Road would suddenly collapse on top of us. Yet we persisted until we finally met a door. Curious, but worried, we opened it slowly. Much to our dismay, we

One prank at Clarke involved three buddies (Cameron MacWhinnie, Larry Farovitch, and Mike Maciolek) and me. We lifted our classmate Linda Kessler's Volkswagen Beetle and carried it to the front door of Rogers Hall. In this picture, I'm in front, looking at the camera.

realized we had crawled all the way to Gawith Hall—where Miss Numbers lived. What if she caught us? We started imagining what her reaction would be if she stood in front of us at the door. The thought was too horrific, so we ran back above ground to our dorm, our clothes stained with dirt. We were fortunately never caught. A couple of years later the school covered the hole.

In the winters, we boys sometimes snuck up to the rooftop of Hotel Northampton on King Street and threw snowballs at the cars and people down below. It was so fun to watch the drivers and pedestrians trying to figure out who the perpetrators were. This continued until the hotel manager finally caught us one day as we tried to go up the stairs.

Many times I would ask, or even coerce, one of the boys to go to the store and buy candies for me when I couldn't do it myself. I had to have at least one piece of candy in my mouth daily, or I would simply die. Even when I played in basketball games, I brought candy with me. One time when I went home for the holidays, my father got a call from the dentist informing him that I had thirteen cavities. Ironically, my maternal grandfather, Edward A. Doherty, was a dentist, who wore dentures. From that point on, my displeased father and mother reminded me constantly to brush my teeth daily. Also, dormitory rules forbade food in our rooms, but I regularly snuck in peanut butter, marshmallow fluff, and a loaf of bread to make sandwiches at night. I often got away with this and other mischief because my blue eyes gave people the sense that I was innocent and naïve.

I don't think even my friends realized just how intense my love of sweets was at first. One evening Gordon snuck into my bedroom and looked into my drawer. His jaw dropped as he saw what I had stashed in there: candies and jars of peanut butter and marshmallow fluff. Gordon reluctantly confessed to me what he had found in the hopes that I would share a sandwich with him. Of course that never happened, because I wasn't going to share my stash.

My peers were sport-minded, so we often went out and played all kinds of sports to kill time after lunch. We faithfully read the sports section of the daily newspapers, building up our love of sports, especially for the Boston Red Sox. Another favorite activity was ice-skating behind Gilmore Gymnasium. Mr. Henry Wilhelm, a long time physical education teacher, coach, and driving teacher who served as a mentor to many of the boys, would water the tennis court with a fire hose every other evening, even when it was freezing outside. He never once complained, always delighted to keep the kids entertained with a smile.

At the beginning of my last year at Clarke—ninth grade—my class got in trouble because we were seriously unmotivated and unfocused on our studies. In fact, we were warned that we would be held back for another year if things didn't change, in hopes that we would shape up. In reality, we were more than ready to move on. In fact, we could have left a couple of years earlier, but it was Clarke's practice to have students remain at school until graduation regardless of readiness. Keep in mind that most teachers spent at least fifty percent of the time trying to correct our speech rather than teaching—how could we not be restless and bored?

Class Trip to Washington, DC

One of the best memories of my school years was our ninth-grade trip to the U.S. Capital. Civics was my favorite school subject; I earned an A on my term paper about John F.

Kennedy and his presidency. I always kept up with what was happening around the world, especially John F. Kennedy's campaign for the presidency of the United States, by reading the Springfield Republican newspaper every morning. It was a dream of mine to visit the U.S. Capitol, the White House, and the Washington Monument. I had seen these landmarks on my family's black-and-white television and in the newspapers, but never in person. I had never even been outside the state. The only trips my family ever took were our annual summer jaunts to Cape Cod.

When I found out that our class would travel to Washington, DC in May 1963, I was ecstatic. I fantasized of meeting fellow Bay Stater President Kennedy during our tour at the White House. I began excitedly making plans, exploring maps, and learning everything I could about each landmark we would visit.

Just before the trip, we received a letter from Gallaudet College (now University) inviting my class to visit the campus. Established in 1864, Gallaudet is the only liberal arts university for deaf people in the world, and is located in Washington, DC, not too far from the U.S. Capitol. However, the university supported the use of sign language. In fact, my classmate Gordon had a brother, who also graduated from Clarke, attending the university at the time.

Initially, the letter was withheld from our class. Upon learning of the invitation from a Gallaudet student, we demanded that our senior advisor and English teacher explain why the letter had been withheld from us, reminding her that it was a federal crime to do this when the letter had been addressed specifically to us. The teacher, outnumbered, responded that it was because the principal didn't want us to visit a "signing school." This was an epiphany for me. Up until then, I hadn't really understood the magnitude of the school's restrictions; I thought that was just how school was. But now it dawned on me that the Clarke staff might not have always had good intentions, and I began to question their actions and lack of respect. Why would they deny Gordon the opportunity to visit his own brother while in the same town?

I couldn't understand Clarke's decision, but I also had no desire to visit this deaf college. Despite this epiphany, I had been thoroughly indoctrinated by Clarke on how horrible sign language was for us. This decision was made was in our best interests, after all, wasn't it? So why would we want to visit Gallaudet?

Brushing the Gallaudet debacle aside, I was very excited about the trip. When I first arrived, the view of the city was surreal. Standing there in front of the U.S. Capitol was deeply thrilling; it was incredible to stand on the very spot where so many world leaders and past presidents had stood, especially before this magnificent building. We had the privilege of sitting in the Visitors' Gallery and witnessing legislative sessions taking place on the floors of both the House and the Senate chambers. We also met with Massachusetts Senator Everett Saltonstall and even Federal Bureau of Investigation Director J. Edgar Hoover. I could see Mr. Hoover's thin lips, and was in awe of how he spoke—but understood not a word. His lips barely moved, and he had a very inexpressive face. We didn't understand what Senator Saltonstall said either. But it didn't matter; we were in the nation's capital!

As we watched the legislators in the chambers, I kept thinking, "There's no way we could ever be deaf and appointed to serve our people. It's impossible." I also thought about how the world belonged to hearing people, and how we Clarke students needed to assimilate

During our class trip, it was difficult to speechread FBI Director J. Edgar Hoover, because he barely moved his lips when he spoke. I'm third from left.

as much as possible. Why did I come to that conclusion in my young fertile mind at that time? The answer now is obvious, but it wasn't back then. It was because we were never exposed to, nor did we ever meet, any deaf adults who had succeeded in life. Throughout all of my schooling years at Clarke, hearing people ran the school. We had not even one deaf role model on campus. Of course I thought we wouldn't succeed if we were deaf.

Throughout the trip, our three chaperones expected us to lipread every word the tour guides said, without any assistance. We students did what we knew best: nod our heads and smile, pretending to understand every word. We spoke to each other, of course, but we didn't understand anything else. Needless to say, we missed out on so much, especially the fascinating history of our beloved country.

Upon our return, we began preparations for our graduation and subsequently our entrance into the real world. The Class of 1963 commencement exercises were held in the Gilmore Gymnasium on June 12, 1963. U.S. Congressman Silvio O. Conte of Massachusetts gave the commencement address while I gave the welcome address; little did I know that this was only the beginning of our encounters, and that our paths would cross again. Ironically, the graduating class and deaf audience members had no access to Congressman Conte's, or the other speakers', message because no interpreters were provided. Instead, we sat and smiled as we looked at each other, or analyzed people's faces and bodies.

CHAPTER 4
An Outsider at Home

My family in approximately 1955. From left, Ward, me, Mom, Bruce (in back), Dad, and Maureen.

Like many others who came from hearing families and attended residential schools, life at home during breaks from school wasn't easy. As the only deaf person in the family—aside from my hard of hearing sister, who I wasn't really close to—I was constantly left out and isolated.

Between the ages of four and seventeen, I lived at Clarke and had little contact with my family, which didn't help our relationship much. Back in those days, Clarke, like many other residential schools, only let students go home for occasions such as Thanksgiving, Christmas, Easter, and summer. Two or three times a year, my parents would visit me on a Sunday and take me out to dinner at Log Cabin on top of Mount Holyoke. At the table, we usually looked or smiled at each other, but there was no real conversation. For example, when I was seven years old, I asked my mother at one of these dinners, "Why are you so big in the belly?" She replied, "Oh, I ate too many blueberry pies!" She was actually pregnant with my sister Maureen, but apparently she thought I wouldn't be able to understand what pregnancy was.

Throughout my life, I always felt like an outsider with my family. I sometimes reluctantly asked my brothers and sister to interpret for me at home, but they usually didn't have the patience to do this. They would make annoyed or disgruntled faces every time I asked them to repeat or clarify what someone said, even if it was a television show (closed captioning did not exist until the 1980s). They often said the much-dreaded "I will tell you later" when I asked what was being said. During meals, I sat at the end of the L-shaped design of the table, facing the kitchen cabinet. This meant I couldn't communicate with or watch the family's conversations—and when I could see them, I had a hard time understanding, often because I had missed the beginning of their conversations. Instead, I focused on my food and left the table as soon as I could.

My oldest brother didn't feel comfortable having me around when he hung out with his friends. He usually got upset when our mother asked him to take me along. Every time I tried to talk, my brother made faces and shushed me with a finger on his lips. One day, Mother forced my brother to take me along to play baseball at a nearby sandlot. My brother was mad so he put me on first base, a difficult position requiring a lot of focus. I wanted to prove to everyone that deaf people could play just like anyone else. In the middle of the game, my brother suddenly grabbed the ball and threw as hard as he could at me. Luckily, I saw the ball flying directly toward me at what seemed like a hundred miles per hour directly toward me, so I immediately raised my father's 1940 baseball mitt in front of my tightly-shut eyes, praying it'd land safely there. I felt a strong thud as the dust from the glove flew all over my face. I slowly opened my eyes and found the ball in my glove for the third out! Relieved, I grinned as the players slapped my back. My brother didn't say a word as he walked away.

Relatives and family friends frequently came to the house for social gatherings, reunions, holiday celebrations, and other events. They always told stories, laughed, and chatted—all as I sat off to the side. Relatives wouldn't take time to chat with me; rather, they'd say superficial things like, "Good to see you. Do you like the food? How is school? You look handsome." Once in a while they tried to get me involved in the conversation, but it made me uneasy because they obviously were doing it out of politeness rather than sincereity interest. I often felt like a dog being patted on the head, so I usually went upstairs to my room and read a book.

What was obvious to me was that my family felt uncomfortable when I talked at home or in public. They constantly told me to keep my voice down or to hush, especially in public. Needless to say, this hurt my feelings, and my self-esteem plummeted. I was very sensitive to criticism about my speech, feeling like a failure during those moments—after all, this was what Clarke emphasized that we needed to do—and then being unable to articulate my thoughts or feelings clearly thereafter. It was painful when my brothers and sister pretended not to be related to me, like my brother did when we went to high school together. He would only nod and say "hey" in the hallway, but would never take it a step further.

Given my love of chatting with people of all ages, especially adults, I always struggled with why my family rarely conversed with me. I was always thirsty for new ideas, information, and news. There were only a very few people in my home life who would take the time to chat with me: our long-time maid Mary Soars (who always let me lick the chocolate frosting from the mixing bowl), family friend Lena Croke (who allowed me to drive her car around town without a license, and also taught me how to make mashed potatoes that later would become a favorite with my children), Aunt Mary Washburn (who would talk to me about anything), and Cousin Betsy Washburn Zito (whose favorite story was that I once locked her in the bathroom and she screamed even though she heard me laughing). With anyone else in the family, I had to make the first move to try and start a conversation—which was always tiresome.

To alleviate my frustrations, I would sneak out of the house and drive over to Boston to visit my long-time schoolmate, Gordon, whose family was deaf. Every time I arrived at the Bergans' home, Gordon was always eager to show the work he had done on his Volkswagen Beetle. Frankly, this didn't matter to me. I often would walk past Gordon and go into the house to chat with his mother, Helen. I was thirsty for news and human connections. Helen was among my role models, because she was very involved with the Clarke School Alumni Association as well as the deaf community for many years. Besides, she actually took time out to talk with me, even if we both didn't use sign language. It was so easy to converse with her; she made me feel as if I was worth her time.

My parents never suspected that I drove to Boston from time to time. One time a police officer stopped me for speeding after a visit at the Bergans' house, and I worried about how my parents would react. Just as the officer was about to issue a ticket, I politely congratulated him for being the first person to catch me speeding. The officer smiled as if proud of this accomplishment, and let me go with a warning. I let out a sigh of relief, thinking my parents would never know about this. A few days later, my father received a notice in the mail about the warning. Oops—I had forgotten that the car was registered to Bob, who wasn't very amused.

Once in a while, I got a ride in Gordon's Volkswagen Beetle. His speedy driving habits made me nervous. He loved to pass cars even when there were cars approaching from the opposite direction! As I freaked out, screaming, Gordon would pat my leg, saying, "Kevin, relax, don't worry, we will make it." I never got used to his driving.

When driving to Red Sox games, Gordon had no patience, especially when stuck in traffic. Instead of waiting for the traffic to move, he would drive on the sidewalk in the city, forcing fans to get out of his way! This embarrassed me so much, but I loved watching all of the fans' angry expressions and shaking fists. That was how Gordon lived life: with no fear or emotions—unlike me. I admired his gutsy nature, but don't think I could ever have been like him!

With Clarke friends on Round Hill Road. I'm the fourth person from right.

I also frequently visited another chum from Clarke, Ray Smith, who lived only fifteen minutes away. Ray's father worked as a salesperson for my father at Saart Bros. Silversmith Co. I often spent time with friends at their homes rather than at my own home, because my family rarely would come and say hi whenever my friends came over.

Two activities helped ease my loneliness at home. The first was the six weeks I spent every summer at our family home in Harwichport, Cape Cod. The beach just down the street helped me stay busy. This continued for fifteen years until my mother was diagnosed with lupus. The other activity was golf; I enjoyed playing golf as well as working as a caddy at the Highland Country Club in Attleboro, where my parents also golfed. These were pleasurable distractions from the loneliness I felt in my own living space.

Every time I was home, I was always eager to return to Clarke, a place I considered my real home with my friends. I once told my father right before returning to Clarke, "Thank you for the wonderful vacation!" Bob visibly didn't like this, and replied quickly, "No need to thank me, you are part of the family." Still, this was how I felt around my family—never fully a part, a feeling that continues to this day.

CHAPTER 5

High School Years

I played as a defensive guard for the Attleboro High football team in 1965.

Clarke's mission always was to help its students assimilate into society—the society that could hear, that is. That meant the students, upon completion of eighth or ninth grade, were to return to their hometowns to attend their local high schools. In my last year, my parents met with Mr. Stanford Blish, the guidance counselor, to discuss my transition into high school. The idea of attending a boarding school was discussed, something I didn't want to do but was reluctant to express. After all, Clarke had trained me to listen to and respect teachers and adults' decisions at all times, regardless of whether I agreed or not. We students knew the consequence for disagreeing or arguing with a person of authority: punishment, even for saying one simple word. This created an influx of passive, accepting students entering "society."

Decisions Without My Input

It took me a while to finally open my mouth and ask, "Why? I'd prefer to go to Attleboro High as I know some friends there. If I go to a prep school, I wouldn't know anyone there. I'm tired of having been away from home since I was four." I knew that high school would be a lot worse if I went to a town where I knew no one, as opposed to attending Attleboro High. At least in Attleboro I knew and hung around with some of my parents' friends' children during the holidays and summers. Bob looked at me and replied, "You are right. I think it's time for you to return home and attend Attleboro High." For the very first time, I had expressed my wish—and got what I wanted, although I had mixed feelings about leaving my friends and familiar surroundings.

Mr. Blish accompanied me on a tour of Attleboro High. As he discussed my courses with the high school counselor, I looked on passively without any input. They glanced at me from time to time, as if I were a young child, and smiled or winked at me—even though I was seventeen years old. Remember, Clarke wouldn't let students graduate until they were sure we were ready, regardless of our ages.

I was informed I would take Latin I, English II, Algebra I, World History, and Physical Education. Looking back, I can't imagine how I managed Latin class without an interpreter. As a Catholic, I was expected to read the Bible as well as watch the priest speak in Latin every Sunday at my hometown church as well as the church in Northampton. I even served as an altar boy at the age of 12 while vacationing in Harwichport. At that time, I had no concept of what Mass was, or the purpose of serving; I simply went along with everyone else.

Gaining Acceptance Through Football

On my first day at Attleboro Senior High, I was uneasy—I was facing a whole new culture after thirteen years in a sheltered environment. During my years at Clarke, I had very limited exposure to the media and the world, even though I had read the paper daily. Reading about the world was different from actually being in it. As I walked into the school, I felt like a stranger in a foreign place without appropriate services or survival skills, not knowing which way to go. At first the other students didn't want to come in contact with me, as if deafness were contagious. Even worse, at the age of seventeen, I was placed with fourteen-year-old students in the sophomore class. This itself was humiliating enough, so I often lied to my friends saying that I was only sixteen. I figured that if I confessed every Sunday in church, that would excuse my lying.

To start making friends, I decided to go out for football. I didn't know which position I wanted to try out for, and thought maybe halfback would be good. But the assistant football coach told me to try out for the linebacker position. To avoid conflict, I agreed and said, "Okay."

The word, "Okay," was a word I used thousands of times throughout my life. Again, I had been taught to accept whatever an adult said and not to disappoint anyone. And once more, I didn't want to be different from others, so I tried very hard to protect my image. I often would plaster on a phony smile and act as if I was onboard with whatever someone said, even if I didn't want it.

I remember vividly one hot day at football practice when I saw a varsity player come over and pick up one of the freshmen players' water bottle and pee in it. Later, during a water break, a freshman drank from this bottle, his face showing his horror when he realized what he had just swallowed. This upset me; I had never felt so vulnerable until that moment. This, to me, was an indication of how the real world was; I finally saw how things were after seventeen years of isolation and naiveté. I didn't want to be the next victim, and knew I was an easy target. Even though I felt bad for the skinny freshman, I acted as if it was no big deal because of my fear of losing friends, or not making the team.

Another difficult lesson for me was how the players swore and used profane language, idioms, and dirty slang throughout practice sessions. Incredibly, even at my age, I didn't know or understand any of the words because nobody at Clarke had ever used such words. Heck, I didn't even know what the middle finger meant—that was how sheltered I had been. Yet, once again, I pretended to understand what the players were saying to avoid looking like a fool. I would see the others looking at me waiting for my reaction, so I'd whisper or mouth what they had said. Fortunately, such words were easy to understand even by hearing people. This helped the others accept me, laughing and slapping my back in delight over my good sportsmanship. Yet I still had no idea what the words meant for the first few days. I didn't dare ask my father or brothers, so instead, I went to the library to look up the definitions and asked my deaf friends. When I found out, I was mortified, but realized I had so much to learn still.

A week after school started, I was placed on the junior varsity team, much to my chagrin. I was now playing alongside fourteen-year-old players, and I felt ridiculous because the younger players kept treating me as if I were dumb. They would grin and say, "Hi," holding their thumbs up to mean "good job," and nothing more. No conversations or anything of substance—just like my family members. I had no idea what in the world the coaches said during games, pep talks, or practices. I simply followed the players wherever they went, like a little duck following its mother.

During the first junior varsity game, the coach had me play as a defense middle guard. Still steaming about being placed with younger kids, I stared right at the center player's eyes. When the ball was snapped, I rammed into the center player, flattening him backwards over the quarterback. This caused the quarterback to lose his balance and I found it easy to knock him over hard, holding him down for a few seconds until the referee tapped my shoulder. Even though I was deaf, I could hear when the referees blew their whistles, but I pretended not to hear them—without penalty. I would always say to the referee apologetically, "Oh, sorry! I didn't realize the play stopped," while pointing at my ear. (I had stopped wearing my hearing aids within the first week of high school, because I didn't want to be different from my hearing peers.)

The quarterback was furious at me for flattening him; he could hardly breathe, given how much bigger I was. I did it again, three times in a row, with multiple players failing to block me. I was too quick—the quarterback never had a chance to even lift his arm for a pass. During the last tackle, I hit the quarterback so hard that he was injured. Apparently, the opposing coach complained to the referee, and I was taken out of the game at the end of the first quarter. The next day the coach told me that I was now a varsity player, first-string. I was elated! After only one week of hard work, I had proven myself. I started most games for two years until I tore the cartilage in my right knee during a game.

As a senior, I could no longer play football because I was nineteen years old (state regulations limited high school players to those up to eighteen years old), so I remained with the team as a co-manager. The other co-manager was one of my brothers. During that season, he rarely talked to me and avoided me in every way possible. It was obvious he didn't want people to know I was his brother because I was deaf, which was difficult for me to accept. There was another challenge to being part of the team: the bus rides. The rides were boring because I missed all the jokes and stories among the players and coaches. To add insult to injury, that year was when we won the Bristol County Championship trophy— something I missed out on as a player because of my age.

Facing the Hard Truth

I quickly found out how information was inaccessible for me, unlike at Clarke. Although at Clarke, we weren't given full access because we weren't allowed to use sign language, it was still better than in hearing environments because we understood each other, had strategies in place for communicating with each other, and worked hard to ensure we all could see each other. We had been deluded about the needs for accessible communication and unpracticed in trying new means…so the rude awakening I received at my high school was a shock to my system.

Back in those days, it was common for deaf students to attend hearing high schools without any type of support services, since accessibility laws didn't exist back then. I didn't have a notetaker, interpreters, or captioning. I also had received no preparation, no advice, no suggestions, and no tips. All I had gotten from my Clarke teachers was empty advice with polite smiles as they said, "We are proud of you! Good luck! Do your best!" The school didn't want to hear complaints or negative feedback. In fact, alumni often told Clarke that they were doing just great in school, that they understood everything, even if they didn't. In fact, Clarke encouraged its students to never resort to writing if they were having problems with communication. Instead, they expected students to repeat themselves hundreds of times until the message was clear. I often joke that it is no wonder I had to see my dentist on almost a monthly basis, as a result of constantly grinding my teeth in frustration. The truth is I was brainwashed to always please everyone on earth, and to avoid "looking deaf"—whatever that meant.

Another thing Clarke forbade its students from doing was hanging out or interacting with deaf people who signed. We were trained that the use of sign language was bad and that our speech skills would deteriorate if we signed. Every time signers were spotted in public, the teachers admonished the Clarke students, "Don't look at them!" The teachers also gave the impression that those who used sign language were not smart. This resulted in many Clarke alumni avoiding signers well into adulthood, often to much regret in later years. I consider this a shame; we should be allowed to communicate in whatever mode we prefer, including sign language.

Strategies for Survival

Each day at Attleboro High School, I sat in an assigned seat at the front of the classroom so I could read the teachers' lips. What a joke! I couldn't see students behind me giving answers or asking questions—nor could I understand the teacher, who often would walk around the classroom. If students sat in front of bright windows, I'd be blinded trying to read lips against the glare. I describe it today as if I were Linda Blair's character in The Exorcist, with my head spinning around trying to follow everything.

Instead of drawing attention to myself, I would simply nod all day long to everyone, pretending to understand. Every time a teacher looked at me to make sure I understood, I'd nod with a facial expression indicating I understood. When a teacher or student shared a funny story, I would see everyone else laughing, and pretend to laugh too. I actually credit the development of my acting skills to this lifelong facade. Every single day, I prayed my teacher wouldn't ask me a question. I also often wanted to close my eyes to rest, because it was physically exhausting constantly trying to keep up with everyone's moving mouths and classroom activities. I couldn't, though, because if I shut my eyes for even a few seconds, my teachers would accuse me of not paying attention. I envied other students in class who fell asleep without reprimand.

Even though I nodded, pretending to understand, I despised when hearing people nodded. Typically there were two groups of people—one that was motivated to communicate with deaf people, and another with an initial strong reaction upon discovering that I was deaf and thus nod to try and evade me. Even today, I see this happening—and I use this to my advantage by teasing them. For example, I sometimes will play on hearing people's self-consciousness about communicating with deaf people by covering my ears and saying, "You're talking too loud!" or leaning in close to them and saying, "Excuse me?" They will repeat themselves, forgetting for a minute that I'm deaf! This often elicits embarrassed chuckles from all parties when I remind them.

Again, one of many deaf people's biggest pet peeves that has endured through centuries is being told, "Oh, it was nothing important" or "I'll tell you later." Many hearing people will also tell us that we're lucky we don't have to hear rumors, gossip, profanity, trivial information, and so on. Yet, this is not their decision to make; this is our decision to make. We can decide whether we want to hear this information or not—even if it's just announcements over the public announcement/intercom system. If it is important enough to be communicated from one person to another, it obviously holds some importance.

As at Clarke, I wore a small body aid connected to an ear mold in my right ear. The school and my parents expected me to wear it while attending high school. I put my aid away after a couple of weeks because I felt like someone from outer space when students stared at me, or worse yet, asked me for the score, thinking I was listening to a baseball game or listening to music. Just like any other high school student, I didn't want to be any different from my peers. I had not yet accepted that I was deaf, and I was frustrated by the irritating noise coming through my hearing aid.

In every class, I had to ask a student to take notes—every single day. I would choose someone who was nerdy, studious, or non-sociable because I knew they would do better than someone who was always socializing, or popular. During study hall, instead of studying or preparing for the next class, I had to copy the notes and return it to the notetaker.

Since I didn't always know what was happening in class, I became bored easily. I daydreamed or pulled pranks on students, and even the teachers, too. I sometimes made students laugh while the teacher was lecturing, embarrassing them at times. When the teacher looked, I put on my "who, me?" face. My getting away with such antics often irritated my classmates, but it was the only way I could stay alert in class.

Without information from class, I had to resort to memorization and extra studying after classes. I could have asked the teacher to repeat for clarification, but that wouldn't have been ideal because I would have asked fifty times per class, annoying everyone else. I also felt humiliated if I had trouble grasping the concept of something, even though it wasn't because I wasn't intelligent; it was because I didn't have full access to the information. To save face, I remained quiet most of the time. Instead of asking for help, I chose to double down on my studying after school and go the extra mile in reading my textbooks and notes. It also usually took me hours upon hours to complete homework, since I had to basically start from ground zero each time. Tests were the bane of my existence, because I didn't want to fail and have my peers look down at me or mock me. For example, every Friday, my English teacher would give the class a spelling/vocabulary test of 25 words. I had to not only memorize the words, but also study the pronunciation and lip movements—which was next to impossible, given how similar some words looked on the lips. Did I really learn new words? Not a chance. The only courses I enjoyed were history and government, since I read the newspaper daily and kept up with politics.

Attempts at a Social Life

Like any other teenager, I was eager to go out with my friends, even though they weren't necessarily genuine friends. I wanted so much to be accepted by my peers because I had nowhere else to go. Many times I wished I could pick up the phone and chat with a friend or ask a girl out on a date. This, of course, wasn't going to happen; relay services didn't exist back then. Imagine me asking my mother or siblings to call a girl for me? Or worse yet, my parents relay my message to a girl: "I love you?" No way!

Even so, many times I had no choice and would ask my siblings, but they'd always make faces of disgust or annoyance. This caused me to stop asking them. I instead made plans while at school. My age made for uncomfortable situations sometimes, though, such as during the season I was too old to play football. The teammates would ask me to join them someplace, when in reality their motive was to get me to buy beer for them (the legal age then was eighteen). I always ended up as their chauffeur as they drank. I wasn't too pleased about this, but I did it, anyway, because I felt I couldn't afford to lose my friendships with them.

Even though I was by nature an outgoing person, I was also shy. Girls sometimes would approach me and ask for a date. I wasn't attracted to some of them, but the major problem was that I couldn't bring myself to say, "No, thank you." I was afraid of offending them. Besides, it showed my friends that deaf people could date just like them. In my last year, a red-haired girl begged me to take her out on a date. I finally agreed, and we went on a double date to a drive-in theater. During the movie, the other couple kissed in the backseat, while I kept my eyes glued to the screen. I was too bashful to make a move, even though I had kissed girls before. Besides, with a hearing girl, it was different story, especially with the communication barriers. The girl, tired of waiting, leaned in and kissed me all over my face and neck. I sat there letting her do that so she would be happy. As she kissed me, I felt her make a noise, so I quickly turned on the overhead light in the car. "What did you just say?" I asked. She scowled as if I were a jerk, and said, "Nothing! Turn the light off!"

Linda, my wife, has never forgotten how I looked in saddle shoes, as shown here; they were all the rage back then.

A few minutes again, I felt the noise again, so I turned the light on again. She again was annoyed, and told me to turn it off again. The couple in the backseat was unhappy, too, because I had interrupted their private time. The next day, I was stunned to see a few spots on my neck, and tried desperately to scrub them off with soap to no avail. It was much later on in life that I realized the noises had been her moaning!

To show my peers that I was just like them, I played baseball and also was the basketball manager. This kept me busy, rather than going nuts at home in isolation. As a senior, I auditioned and got a small part as a bellhop in "Born Yesterday" with two lines: "Good morning," and "Thank you."

I'm rehearsing for my high school play, "Born Yesterday" in this picture, with classmateTom McAvoy.

This thrilled me, because I had loved acting since I was a little child. I always loved to watch Laurel and Hardy, The Three Stooges, and I Love Lucy given their ample facial expressions and physical antics that minimized the need for captioning. Fortunately, I had a wonderful public speaking teacher, Paul Kelly, who was one of the rare ones who felt comfortable communicating with me. He encouraged me in everything I did and I appreciated his confidence in me.

A Defining Moment

My sophomore year, there was an assembly at school for a University of Massachusetts band performance. Since I couldn't understand anything at any of the assemblies, I often chose to instead examine the people in the audience, their outfits, and their expressions. Suddenly, the music stopped and the principal came onstage to make an announcement. I saw how everyone's faces dropped, and they quietly left the auditorium with long faces. I had no idea what was going on, and went to the locker room to change for football practice. I had a funny feeling that something wasn't right. I noticed how the players kept talking to each other sadly, so I finally asked a player what happened. "You didn't hear anything about President Kennedy?" the player asked. I said no, and the player pointed a finger to his temple. "President Kennedy was shot and he died an hour ago." It was November 22, 1963.

I was shocked. "Are you telling me that President Kennedy was shot?" The player nodded, and I kept asking all kinds of questions, trying to comprehend what I had been just told. Kennedy had been my idol for a long time. Practice was canceled, and we went home. I felt isolated, empty, and upset about being the last person to find out in the school. That was a defining moment in my life, one that I continue to remember vividly even today.

Getting Ready for Graduation

By my senior year, I was unsure of my future. Back then, any student who had a disability had to report to a vocational rehabilitation (VR) agency. I was assigned to a VR counselor who had no training working with deaf people. The counselor tested me, including an aptitude test, and recommended that I work as an assembler in a factory. He noted that I had good and quick hands. "Hey, Kevin, you will make a lot of money!" he said with a patronizing smile. When I got home and told my father about the counselor's comments, Bob went through the roof and gave the counselor a piece of his mind. Our family members were well-educated, and Bob wanted that for me as well.

My college-educated family expected me to follow in their footsteps. The problem was I didn't know what field or career I wanted. I had never been exposed to a variety of careers and didn't even know what the options were. I applied to Dean Junior College, in nearby Franklin, to major in general education. Meanwhile I asked my friend Gordon about his plans. Gordon chose to follow in his brother's footsteps and attend Gallaudet College. I had mixed feelings about Gordon's decision, since Gallaudet used sign language as its primary mode of instruction. I reminded Gordon that Clarke would be very disappointed if he went there. Yet, later on, I realized, "Why should we allow Clarke to make decisions for its alumni?!"

Today, I hold very little memory of my graduation day in June 1966, for two reasons. The first reason was I missed all that was said, including my name being called to get my diploma. In fact, the only reason I knew it was my turn to go onstage was because our names were called in alphabetical order. At the time, I was proud about my ability to figure this out; but now as I look back on it, what a joke!

The second reason is starker: my parents attended my graduation, but none of my siblings or relatives did. I had learned very little academically, but had acquired a lot of real-world knowledge through my socialization with peers, even as difficult as that was. My high school years made me stronger, and more independent, despite all the challenges—as frustrating or embarrassing as they were—and I was ready to face the real world.

CHAPTER 6
College: A New Frontier

The National Technical Institute for the Deaf's pioneer class in 1968. I am in the second row from top, fourth from left.

After receiving my high school diploma—worth $.10 to me—I attended Dean Junior College in Franklin, Massachusetts, a two-year college about a thirty-minute drive from home. The college experience was very similar to what I went through high school: no support services, little social life given the lack of peers I could easily communicate with like my deaf friends, limited communication, and so on. Still, I was more prepared than I had been when I started high school.

I again went out for football so I could start making new friends. Assistant coach Dale Lippert was willing to work with me to keep me in the loop during practices and games, and during the off-season, too. The head coach, for some reason, didn't have the confidence—or perhaps the time—to communicate with me, so he relied on Lippert to relay messages. This wasn't always successful, though. Once, while I was playing defense Lippert gave me the wrong play, and I went left when all of the players went right and knocked me down flat! During my second year at school, Garry Scutt from Birmingham, New York, joined the football team. For some reason, Scutt became interested in me and helped me in many ways, always making sure I was included. For example, when my teammates talked to me, he made them take their helmets off—which was comical, but helpful. Scutt later went on to Northern Michigan University, and was drafted to the Green Bay Packers in 1974. He is now retired after 38 years of teaching and coaching.

The college atmosphere was family-like, very friendly. Even though the students and staff were great, I once again had to make the first move to begin conversations. As in high school, I used my sense of humor as a way of breaking the ice. For example, I enjoyed the extra attention during my first year after I told people I was a foreigner, explaining my accent. I proudly said, "I am a Russian. I come from Moscow!" This was when the Cold War between the United States and Russia was in full force. I also told people I knew several languages, and silently chuckled when their eyes widened as they said, "Wow! That's amazing!" I also often saw others whisper to each other, "Hey, this guy is from Russia."

Since it was a two-year school, I had to search for other colleges to complete my bachelor's degree studies. I received a letter from Clarke School President Dr. George Pratt announcing the new National Technical Institute for the Deaf (NTID) in Rochester, New York. In 1965, U.S. President Lyndon B. Johnson signed the National Technical Institute for the Deaf Act into law. This bill established a postsecondary institute for technical education for people who were deaf and hard of hearing at the Rochester Institute of Technology.

The letter from Dr. Pratt encouraged Clarke alumni to consider attending this new school, however I was surprised and confused because Clarke kept telling us not to mix or hang around with signers. So I drove to visit Dr. Pratt in his office, expressing my confusion. He replied, "Oh, this is a hearing college, you can hang around with hearing people instead of the signers." When I look back now, I think to myself, "Why did I have to ask for his opinion instead of making my own decision?" Of course I knew the answer: I was never taught to make my own decision or express my opinion until I entered NTID!

During this time period, as I grew older and wiser, the division between my hearing and deaf worlds had grown sharper. Even so, I still didn't accept that I was deaf; I preferred to socialize with hearing people, having been programmed by Clarke and the people in my life that I had to assimilate into the hearing society. As a result, I looked down on deaf people who signed, finding myself embarrassed by them. I did everything possible to not be like "them."

Yet, despite all my indoctrination and efforts, I still struggled with my identity as a deaf person. I was tired of being confused about my needs and what I wanted to be, but I knew I wanted to be accepted for who I was instead of trying to accommodate everyone's expectations. So I built up the courage to see about transferring to this new college in New York. I also wanted to know what it would be like to have full access among people like me, to meet deaf professionals who I could emulate, and to learn much more. Excited to see how close Rochester was to New York City, I looked at a New York map. After a few minutes, I still couldn't find the town…and then I looked farther away from the city. Oh, no! The city was actually closer to Niagara Falls and Toronto, a full six hours from NYC. That dashed any and all hopes I had of painting New York City red.

A New Era

I was accepted and began at NTID in September 1968 as one of its first 70 students. The campus, part of the Rochester Institute of Technology (RIT), had recently relocated from downtown Rochester to the farmland swamps of Henrietta. When we new students arrived, the campus's universal use of red bricks that eventually led to its nickname of "Brick City" wasn't complete yet, new trees were planted everywhere, and its renowned campus paths had not been built yet. Before NTID's buildings were completed in 1974, students had to walk from their dorms to academic buildings along a walkway known as the Quarter Mile. This walk was brutal for many because of the wintry weather and high winds. At the tender age of 20, I had already started to bald, so I had taken to wearing a toupee. Each day as I walked the Quarter Mile, I held onto my toupee tightly. One day, one of the other original students, Guy Wonder from Washington, took me to a wig shop and had me fitted with a toupee that fit better— but not before we spent four long hours in the shop!

Still undecided about a career, I reluctantly chose business administration, even though I had no interest in it. After all, business was what my father and brothers had done. On the first day, there was a gathering in an auditorium. NTID Director Robert Frisina told the 70 pioneering students in sign language that "we were in a fishbowl" because we were part of what NTID referred to as the "Grand Experiment," to see whether or not deaf students could get a good college education in technical fields with hearing people. Fifty years later, Frisina said that he was proud to witness the success of the "Grand Experiment," and that "NTID is remarkable for its epic role in the history of deaf people, creating technical and professional career opportunities, inspiring changes in educational practices and enabling socioeconomic parity for individuals who are deaf."

I remember how cleverly Frisina convinced Congress that our NTID academic building (later named the Lyndon Baines Johnson building) needed an air conditioning system even though we were in cool Rochester, and the other RIT buildings didn't have air conditioning: it was because our hearing aid batteries needed to be stored in cool rooms.

At the beginning, I refused to learn sign language because I didn't want to disappoint my parents or Clarke. That, and I didn't want to be like "them"—deaf people who signed. This wasn't a big deal at first, because the campus was full of hearing students and most of the 70 deaf students had grown up without sign language. The turning point for me, though, came when Robert Panara, the first deaf person to be hired as a faculty member at RIT, asked to meet in his tiny office in

48

the General Studies Building. Panara, who was friendly and calm, always with a smile on his face, had heard that I was very interested in acting and theatre. From behind his desk, he said, "Kevin, I understand you wanted to get involved in theatre—but you need to learn sign language first."

I expressed hesitancy at learning sign language. He nodded thoughtfully, and shared his experiences growing up as an oralist in New York. His gentle, kind nature showed through as he said it was when he attended the American School for the Deaf in Connecticut that he learned sign language for a year before attending Gallaudet. I was spellbound by Panara's smooth and clear signing as he said, "Don't worry about your speech . . . you will not lose the quality of speech, let me tell you!" After this talk, I felt a lot better having found someone I could rely on for advice if needed. It was at this point that I began to learn sign language—and realized just how much I had missed out on all those years. It also helped that all of us in the NTID group decided to learn to sign at the same time, because most of us came from oralist backgrounds. We all worked together and I gradually started to sign on a regular basis.

One thing that really turned me around was the available support services such as interpreting, note taking, guidance counseling, and much more. This access opened up the world for me, especially being part of an environment where hearing people were eager to learn how to work with deaf people. I was involved in activities such as student government, leadership workshops, theatre, the Sigma Pi Fraternity, guest lectures, and assemblies—all fully accessible at all times. My mind exploded like a volcano because I at long last could understand what was happening inside and outside classrooms—and more importantly, I could understand all this information without struggle.

Eventually, with the help of Panara, Guy Wonder, Chuck Baird (who went on to become a renowned deaf artist and actor), George Payne, and Fred Gravatt, and me, NTID's first drama club was established in 1969. Panara directed his first production, "The Marriage Proposal," in 1970. My Clarke

classmate
Linda Kessler,
Chuck Baird,
and I were
actors in this
production.
I was also
involved in the
"The Claw,"
"The City
Lights," and
"Laurel and
Hardy" (the
last two with
renowned
actor CJ
Jones).

I served as the first NTID Drama Club's treasurer (I'm the second from right). The officers (shown L-R) were Freddie Gravatt, business manager; George Payne, secretary; Guy Wonder, president; Michael Deninger, advisor; Robert Panara, advisor; Loy Golladay, advisor; and Charles Baird, vice president.

Theater
gave me an
opportunity to express myself,
and this creative outlet developed
my confidence, pride, and
understanding and appreciation
of literary works. Years and years
of faking it, acting, and being
suppressed in expressing myself
all came out on the stage. I also
had the opportunity to participate
in the National Theater of the
Deaf's famed summer program
and work with renowned actors
such as Bernard Bragg, Ed
Waterstreet, Linda Bove, Mary
Beth Miller, Dorothy Miles, Juliana
Fjeld, Phylis Frelich, sisters Jane
and Freda Norman, and director
David Hays. This began a lifelong

I performed with with Charles "CJ" Jones in a Laurel and Hardy skit at NTID. CJ has gone on to become a successful stage and movie actor.

50

career in theater that continues today.

NTID Dean and Director William E. Castle, who took over after Frisina left, was another key individual in my life. A man of small stature,

Dr. William Castle and I met with U.S. Senator Edward Brooke from Massachusetts after I testified at a Congressional hearing.

Castle always wore flamboyant jackets and ties; in fact, Congressman Conte once wore sunglasses when he was at a Congressional hearing with Castle. Castle was very interested in the well-being of both deaf students and staff, and created many opportunities, especially for professional growth. He was very supportive of the performing arts, and also established an art gallery at the college. Both Castle and his wife, Diane, inspired me through their long-time involvement with several deaf organizations as well as education. Castle also asked me to represent the NTID student body at the 1971 U.S. Congressional budget hearing, which was a huge honor. Another student and I flew down to DC, and we met Senator Edward Brooke from Massachusetts, the first African American to be popularly elected to the United States Senate who would later be invited to serve on NTID's National Advisory Group. The experience of the hearing, with interpreters present, was exhilarating and further motivated me to become involved in politics.

My three years at NTID were the best years for me, because I was far more directly involved with students and staff than I had ever been in the past. I also developed a stronger deaf identity, much to my happiness, through daily interaction and living with deaf students. In 1970, I was hired as the first deaf resident advisor on campus, where I was responsible for a mixture of both deaf and hearing students on my floor. It was a life-changing experience in that it was a great privilege to supervise both deaf and hearing students, who saw that deaf people could be in charge. Although the negativity I had encountered all of my life about sign language was misleading, I had appreciated learning how to speak; now I was glad to learn sign language.

A Quick Stint in the Corporate World

As part of my studies, I was to participate in a work-study program. I interviewed with the manager at Xerox Corporation in nearby Webster about the possibility of working as an auditor. At that time NTID encouraged students to have interviews without interpreters because it'd be good practice to not rely on interpreters 24 hours a day. Unfortunately, the interviewer was difficult to lipread. Instead of showing frustration, I acted as if I had no trouble following. When the manager smiled or laughed, I pretended to laugh along with him. At the end, he said to me, "I am so impressed that you understood every word I said!" I smiled and shook his hand. Once again, my acting skills had come to my rescue.

After a week on the job, I immediately knew I could not continue in this field. I hated my job; the office had four walls, and even worse, the clock was right in front of me. I kept looking at the clock waiting for 12:00 p.m. or 4:00 p.m. to strike. I felt as if I worked for twenty-four hours instead of the required eight because the clock moved so slowly. Despite earning a bachelor's degree in business administration in 1971, I realized I preferred to work with people in the education field.

To this day, NTID has been one of the most valuable investments of my life.

CHAPTER 7
The Love of My Life

Linda and I are clearly well in love in this photograph, taken when she visited me during the winter of 1968.

In my last year at Clarke in 1963, I noticed a cute twelve-year-old named Linda Howe from Springfield, Massachusetts, walking upstairs to the middle school second floor daily. In spite of her shyness, she always smiled every time we passed each other. Even though I knew she was too young for my seventeen years, my heart sung, "Linda! Linda! Linda!" I thought she had a beautiful smile, one that she always sent my way whenever we passed each other, although she doesn't remember that. She does remember my 1950s-style black-and-white saddle shoes, though.

A few years later, on New Year's Eve in 1966, I was invited to a tobogganing party at fellow Clarke alumnus and community leader Jack Levesque's home in Monson, Massachusetts. Fate seemed to be on my side; Linda was there, now all grown up, although she was still attending Clarke. She had come with a classmate, Nancy Smith (later

This is the only picture of both Linda and me as students at Clarke; it seems to have been taken in 1960. I'm in the back, while Linda is at far right.

known for owning a hand-woven fabric and designer clothing business in Los Angeles). I was thrilled to see Linda and said hello as she took a bite of a pastry. She shyly said "Hi" as she expressed her dislike for the pastry. I suggested she dump it into a nearby trashcan, which she did. Just then, my friend Bill Brown, who had also attended Clarke and then Dean Junior College, came by and I introduced him to Linda. During this introduction, I shared that Linda didn't care for the pastry and had thrown it away. Bill said he was the one who brought the pastries, and Linda was mortified by this revelation. Not knowing what to say to him, she walked out of the room and joined the others. I thought my chance with Linda had been ruined and that she would never forgive me.

Later that evening, snow blanketed the grounds under the moonlight sky. Five people jumped on a long toboggan and started downhill. I jumped on at the last second, not realizing I had sat behind Linda. She suddenly turned around and gave me a lovely smile that needed no words. Sparks flew, and I knew I was in love. After that party we talked and realized that we shared many interests and values.

Six months later I attended Linda's graduation at Clarke. She introduced me to her parents and relatives, but she didn't yet realize how much I loved her. She did give me a graduation picture of herself though.

I didn't see Linda again until December 16, 1967. I had gotten her address from the school alumni director, and wrote a letter asking her to be my date for a Christmas party that night, but she had already accepted another young man's invitation to that same party. Undaunted, I went alone and sat at the same table with her and her date. When the dancing began, I waltzed Linda away from her date to a small room, where my heart finally spoke.

"Linda, I love you," I spoke. As she read my lips, she was shocked into speechlessness. When I took her into my arms and kissed her, she responded silently but surely. My long-time classmate, Linda Kessler, suddenly entered the room and saw us kissing; she had inadvertently become the first witness of our lifelong partnership.

One month later, I took Linda out to the local tavern bar in Springfield. With candles flickering, I spent a lot of time talking. Linda later admitted she didn't pay much attention as she was too focused on my blue eyes. To this day, Linda tells people that the reason she married me was because of my blue eyes.

I was initially uncomfortable telling my parents about my new love because I was afraid they wouldn't approve of me marrying a deaf girl. Linda's parents, on the other hand, welcomed me with open arms. The one-hour drive from Dean Junior College to Linda's home in Springfield once or twice a month proved that distance brought us closer. In the spring of 1968, I finally introduced Linda to my parents. Much to my surprise, my parents were delighted to meet her. Maybe they were just trying to be polite, not wanting to upset me. Today, I wonder why I was so worried; after all, I was an adult. Why did I need their approval?!

When I transferred to RIT, 400 hundred miles away, this was heartbreaking for both Linda and me. The added distance cut our weekends together down to once a month.

My car, a Volkswagen bug just like Gordon's, became an animal transport unit as I brought Linda a parakeet, a Cairn terrier puppy, and other assorted pets to keep her company in my absence. We faithfully wrote letters back and forth, given that there was no other technology for us to maintain contact. At NTID, a good number of girls were interested in me, but I had no interest in them. I was in love with Linda, and only Linda.

Linda and me on our beautiful wedding day on May 27, 1972.

After Linda graduated from high school, she got a job as a typist at Massachusetts Mutual Insurance Company in Springfield. She begged me to get married so we could be together. I wanted to graduate and get a job first, but worried that I would lose her because it would be another two years. To show both my love and promise, I decided to get an engagement ring. On May 22, 1970, Linda flew to visit me for the weekend in Rochester. I told her that we were invited to a friend's birthday party at a motel near campus. As we entered the room, flashes went off everywhere, blinding Linda, who was clueless to what was happening. I gently told her to look up at a big white ribbon with an engagement ring above the door. She was delighted and shocked, and hugged me. She then looked around and realized so many of our friends were in the room, finally understanding that this was actually an engagement party.

It was a beautiful day on May 27, 1972 when, in front of over one hundred guests at Our Lady of the Sacred Heart Church in Springfield, Massachusetts, I spoke, "Yes, I take thee, Linda Howe, as my lawfully wedded wife," and we were wedded by Father Boland. The reception was held at Knights of Columbus, where band leader Dan Cavanaugh sang an original song he had written for us:

There is a girl in Kevin's life
Today Linda is his wife
They have a beautiful love affair
Linda with the light brown hair

Holding her close in the night
Will bring Kevin a fantastic delight
Everything Kevin has, he will always share
With Linda with the light brown hair

Missing her while they're apart
Brings such pain to his heart

Kevin carries thoughts of Linda everywhere
The girl with the light brown hair

The wedding day was lovely. Everything was just about perfect, but one thing was missing. Much to our disappointment, we had no interpreters for either the Mass or the reception.

We held off on our planned six-week honeymoon of backpacking in Europe that summer, since I had to return to my new job. We instead spent our weekend honeymoon at Mount Airy Lodge in Mount Poconos, Pennsylvania.

CHAPTER 8
Returning to My Roots

I eventually returned to Clarke as a guidance counselor, taking the position over from my former guidance counselor Stanford Blish.

J ust before graduating from RIT in December 1971, I sent applications to 30 schools in the country. None of them were hiring since it was the middle of the school year. By chance, I attended a workshop where a friend introduced me to Kenneth Kritz, the principal of Maryland School for the Deaf (MSD). Kritz had been searching for a person who could teach drama and consumer education class and could start immediately. I reminded him that I wasn't a fluent signer, and he immediately reassured me. "Don't worry about that. We accept all kinds of signers," he said. He was right; I never once felt ostracized or shamed for my signing skills.

Since I had no desire to work in the business world, I jumped at this opportunity. My salary would be $7,000 per year, and my wife Linda would be a teacher aide and typing teacher. She had worked as a typist for Mass Mutual Life

Insurance Company after high school graduation, so this was an ideal transition for her. In January 1972, when I drove to the campus in Frederick, Maryland, I was thrilled to see that the school was located on Clarke Place, which reminded me of my alma mater. Serendipity, perhaps!

MSD at the time practiced total communication, which utilized all communication including sign language, oralism, fingerspelling, written English, and visual aids, depending on each child's needs and abilities. Despite my weakness in signing, I enjoyed teaching, and my students apparently had no trouble following me, citing my clear facial expressions and body language. The new career proved to be a great start for me because of the active and influential faculty surrounding me, who also served as terrific role models for me. Many of them were Gallaudet graduates and national advocates or leaders in the Deaf community, such as Gertrude Galloway, who was an education advocate and the first female president of the National Association of the Deaf; she also later served as superintendent of the New Jersey School for the Deaf.

I served as an assistant football coach, drama advisor, and Junior National Association of the Deaf advisor. It was a turning point in my life, as I finally knew what I wanted to do career-wise: work with students. Immediately after I arrived at MSD, the school encouraged me to take graduate deaf education courses at Western Maryland College (now McDaniel College) in Westminster, an hour away. I had just graduated, and now MSD wanted me to take graduate classes? I didn't have any energy left to continue studying, but my colleagues dragged me to classes nevertheless. Looking back, I'm grateful they did this, because I earned a master's degree in deaf education in 1976.

In 1973, I was the first alumnus to be appointed to the NTID National Advisory Group. It was a rewarding experience because I had the opportunity to meet even more educational advocates and leaders such as George Propp, Robert Sanderson, Frank Sullivan, Fred Schreiber, Larry Newman, Merv Garretson, Ralph White, and Malcolm Norwood, as well as Dr. Richard Thompson. Despite my youth, they all helped me in my professional growth by helping me build my confidence and showing me that if they could do it, I could also do it.

After two and half years at MSD, even with all the outstanding deaf role models and opportunities in Frederick, Linda and I longed to return to our home state of Massachusetts. Dr. Thompson, the founder of the Massachusetts Office of Deafness (the forerunner to today's Massachusetts Commission for the Deaf and Hard of Hearing), who I had served on the NTID Advisory Group with, encouraged me to apply for a job at the Beverly School for the Deaf, a school that employed both total communication and oral approaches. In June 1974, I was offered a teaching position at the Beverly School for the Deaf, where Linda would be a teacher aide. Richard Flint, the school executive director, gave me additional school responsibilities throughout my three years at the school, such as serving as the head of the upper school, dean of students, coordinator of the after-school program, senior advisor, and guidance counselor.

Our Family Expands

When I flew to Rochester for a two-day NTID Advisory Group meeting in early February, Linda was pregnant and due in March. Throughout the entire meeting, I was preoccupied with the pregnancy and Linda's well-being. The morning after I arrived home, on February 8, 1975, Linda's water broke. I immediately drove her to Beverly Hospital at 9 a.m. At 6:30 p.m., an exhausted Linda was wheeled into the delivery room, unable to hold the baby in anymore. The doctor flew in like a superhero from the other room and caught the baby just in time. I was lucky to see the whole thing just as I walked into the room. It was a boy, weighing in at six pounds and nine ounces. It was a proud and emotional time for us both.

Because the baby came a month early, we had not yet made up our minds on what to name the baby. Finally, we decided to name him Kevin Jr. Shortly after the naming, I was shocked to see my parents arrive at the hospital after driving through a fierce snowstorm. I had asked the hospital to call them to let them know of our first child, but never in the world did I expect them to drive over. "Your mother wanted to come over," my dad said. They seemed devoid of emotion or joy as we did not communicate much that night. I do not know what went through their minds as they drove all the way, but I am sure the question of whether Kevin Jr. was deaf or hearing crossed their minds.

As Kevin Jr. grew, we communicated with him as much as possible using our voices. We discovered what he didn't like, such as spaghetti. Maybe it was because Linda had a full plate of spaghetti the night before little Kevin was born. In time, we began to suspect that our now two-year-old had some hearing loss because every time we called him, it took him a while to figure out which direction the voice was coming from. Yet, we figured he could hear because he vocalized and talked a lot. After some time, we took him to an audiologist, and the test results indicated that he had normal hearing. We found that hard to believe, and were disturbed because we thought of other parents who had never been exposed to or worked with deaf babies who might get erroneous results. Such a mistake could seriously delay the child's language learning.

While keeping an eye on Kevin Jr.'s progress, I continued to teach at Beverly School for the Deaf. I worked closely with the school media specialist, Jay Innes, who would later be a professor at Gallaudet University. We both coached basketball together and coordinated the school's summer basketball camp. Ah, poor kids! They frequently got confused with the different communication modes between us two coaches—I often spoke without signing, especially when I was excited, while Jay signed at all times. Imagine what the scene was like when we tried to communicate with the players on the basketball court! One weekend, our team traveled to Clarke School for the New England basketball tournament. Jay Innes was in disbelief to see me communicating orally instead of signing. This was how strongly the school influenced me.

Returning to Rochester

In 1977, I was offered a position at NTID as a career opportunities specialist. It was a hard decision because I didn't want to leave New England, but I felt I at least owed NTID for all the college had done for me. So, our family of three moved to New York and we bought our first home, a ranch house in

Ready to act as Capulet in NTID's Romeo and Juliet play in 1979.

Henrietta, for $29,000. Once we settled down, we decided to take little Kevin to Rochester School for the Deaf for another hearing test. The test showed that he indeed had a 60-decibel loss. He was fitted with two hearing aids right away, and began to take speech lessons at Al Sigl Center (Rochester Hearing and Speech Center).

For the next two years at NTID, I traveled all over the country recruiting, reviewing applications, and dealing with vocational rehabilitation issues in each of the states I visited. I also continued acting, playing Capulet in NTID's production of "Romeo and Juliet." When I met with prospective students or visitors on campus, the prankster in me sometimes came out. I often told them that President Lyndon B. Johnson was buried under the plaque in front of the building that bears his name. People would run to their cars and grab their cameras, and say how lucky they were to see the burial site instead of having to go all the way down to LBJ's hometown in Texas. I never let them know that I had been only kidding.

On December 30, 1977, Linda experienced contractions and was brought to Highland Hospital in Rochester. After a couple of hours, at 4:30 p.m., Kristi Ann was born, weighing seven pounds and twelve ounces. When the nurse placed Kristi Ann on Linda's chest, I touched my daughter for the first time and burst into tears. Little Kevin Jr. was happy to meet his sister when she got home from the hospital. Soon after her birth, we knew unquestionably that Kristi Ann was deaf. We weren't disappointed or excited; we were just thrilled that our children were healthy.

We thought about enrolling both children at our alma mater, the Clarke School. Yet at the same time, we didn't want to send our children so far away from home. We felt strongly that the family should stay together and were about to explore other schools in the Greater Rochester area. When the school discovered we likely wouldn't enroll Kevin Jr. because of the distance, we unexpectedly received the exciting news that we both had been offered jobs at Clarke and a place to live on campus. Admittedly, we were surprised at the job offers because of Clarke School's hiring policy: deaf people weren't allowed to be employed at the school. Despite this archaic policy, a few years earlier Clarke School brought in a deaf art teacher, Winchell Moore—the school's first deaf teacher on campus in more than 75 years. He and his wife Ruth had two sons enrolled at Clarke School.

When Clarke President George Pratt recommended me to the Board of Trustees, one deaf board member strongly opposed my hiring because I had previously taught at schools that used sign language. Despite this, the board supported Pratt's decision to hire me. I began working as a guidance counselor with a $12,000 salary, replacing my very own counselor from my Clarke years, Stanford Blish. Linda was hired as a typing teacher, and we were the first deaf couple ever to be hired at Clarke. We resided in Leonard House, a former dormitory, where Linda first boarded when she was four years old in 1954. We were thrilled to be back at our alma mater school and even better, our children would be living with us. When we arrived at Clarke, the teachers and staff welcomed us with open arms. The atmosphere at the school had changed since I graduated in 1963—for the better.

Choosing Clarke for Our Kids

We are often asked why we would send our children to Clarke School given its oralism philosophy and our negative experiences at the school. One thing to keep in mind is that before the 1970s,

Clarke President George Pratt welcomes Kevin Jr., Linda, Kristi Ann, and me back to the school in 1979.

corporal punishment and oralism were simply commonplace. But during the 1970s, when we started having children, there was a national shift away from both practices, especially at Deaf schools.

As parents, there is an inherent need within ourselves to do the right thing for our children. When Linda and I were considering placing our children at Clarke, we took into consideration the fact that the school's curriculum and resources were top-notch, the students were prepared for mainstreaming, the educational standards were high for all students, and the commitment and dedication that the teachers showed to their students was outstanding. With the departure of Ms. Numbers and most of the staff from our time as students, along with the infusion of new teachers with new philosophies and beliefs, the atmosphere at Clarke was very different from what we had experienced. Instead of a cold, institutional feel, the school felt much more home-like and the staff were more sensitive to the needs of the individual students.

Linda and I had a wide range of experiences, both personal and professional, within different educational

65

environments that used different communication modalities, including ASL. We looked at all of our options and considered each of them carefully when we were deciding which school we wanted to enroll our children in. Ultimately, we felt that Clarke School, with its new staff, better treatment of students, high standards of excellence, top-notch curriculum and resources, and most importantly, the dedicated teachers, was the best fit for our children. It must be noted that a critical component of our children's upbringing was that they had us—so they could always ask us any questions about what it was like being deaf because we clearly knew what they would experience.

Communication is critical for every child regardless of communication methods. The earlier children begin to learn language and practice communicating, the more they can learn each and every day. It's important for children to learn about what's happening around the world, to express themselves, and to think and develop their ideas. This is what distinguished our children's upbringings at Clarke from our own: they had full access. At home, communication was always open, and from the earliest TTY (teletypewriter) and closed captioning devices to conversations at dinner, everyone lived in a fully accessible environment at home. With our children, we gestured and spoke/lipread so we wouldn't confuse them about communication methods, especially since we lived on campus; however, when friends came over, we signed in front of our children. Today, we all sign.

I think it is crucial that families consider all possible educational approaches for deaf children and that parents are given every opportunity to learn about each educational program/philosophy equally. What works for one child may not necessarily work for another child. Linda and I are grateful for the outstanding education our three children received at Clarke School (and even more grateful that it was nothing like our experiences). Yet we are also keenly aware that not every child who attended Clarke has had the same experiences that our children did. We hope that all families with deaf children can find the school that is the best fit for their children.

A Man of Many Hats

For twenty-one years, I served in many capacities in addition to my counselor role at Clarke School. When I first arrived at Clarke, my priority was to form the High School Preparation Program, with the help of Director of Mainstream Program David

Working with Clarke Students Ernie Freyre and Christine Ferriera as a guidance counselor.

Manning. We were to create a program that helped prepare students to begin their mainstream experiences post-Clarke. Based on my personal lack of readiness for high school, I didn't want any other student to face the same obstacles I had. The program was criticial in obtaining support services for the students at their schools.

I organized the school's files and memorabilia to help preserve its historical information, created an alumni museum, chaired a teacher appreciation fundraising campaign, established a student community service program and a mentoring program, coordinated an after-school program and alumni affairs, and encouraged the creation of an oral interpreting program to help prepare the students for high school. I also taught both U.S. government and health education classes.

Throughout our years at Clarke School, Linda and I always encouraged parents to give their deaf children love, support, affection, attention, patience, and 24-hour communication access, and perhaps more importantly, be open-minded. This was based on my own experiences growing up in a communication-deprived family and recognizing the importance of connections with each other.

Despite Clarke's strict oral philosophy, the school was open to my input and found itself in a better position than

67

ever before. For example, TTYs were installed in every department, and oral interpreting and closed-captioned services were provided for meetings, workshops, drama plays, graduation ceremonies, and field trips. In the age before texting or video technology, I was provided with oral interpreting services for phone calls. One

I was privileged to introduce Massachusetts Lieutenant Governor Evelyn Murphy to Clarke School students and staff when she was running for governor.

of my pet peeves, however, was that the secretary or whoever interpreted for me would frequently hold a long conversation on the phone, but only give me a brief summary at the end. When relay services were finally established, it was a huge blessing for me, for now I no longer had to depend on others to make calls.

A funny incident took place the second week of a new school year. The school had a fire drill. Although it was a school for deaf students, there were no visual fire alarms. The entire building was vacated, except for one person: me. I was working at my desk without any clue. Afterward, I could not help but wonder if Clarke was trying to get rid of me in the event of a fire! Needless to say, the school heard from me about that incident and quickly added visual fire alarms to every classroom to make sure that it didn't happen again.

One of my least favorite duties was to attend Individualized Education Plan (IEPs) meetings. It was very tiring to lipread everyone at the meeting, including the oral interpreters, especially after the day's long hours. On top of that, my supervisor sometimes gave a canned and incredibly dull report to parents. During one IEP meeting, due to the lack

68

of windows, the room was stuffy and warm, making it difficult for me to keep my eyes open. I could have fallen asleep, but the upper school supervisor, Michael O'Connell, sat next to me and noticed under the table how my socks had fallen. He quickly reached down and harshly tugged at my leg hair. Not knowing what was happening, I yelped in pain. All the meeting attendees jumped at my scream. They all stared at me in confusion, and I felt chastened. O'Connell realized that he was now on my target list and was worried every time he saw me after that he'd fall victim to one of my infamous pranks.

I always strove to make the students feel special and welcomed when they visited my office. I wanted to instill the self-confidence and the can-do attitude that I had always lived by. I really believed in my students, and held high standards for them. I could clearly understand and verbalize what the students were feeling, their fears, confusion, and concerns about anything in their lives. Often, students would tell their classroom teachers that they had personal problems and needed to see the counselor, but really they were bored in class and just wanted to have a chat with me. I was always fine with that.

Fun Times

I was a chaperone during a senior trip to Washington, DC in 1980, sharing a hotel room with another chaperone, upper school supervisor Robert Storm. The next day, Robert was cranky all day thanks to my deep and loud snoring the night before. I also often talked in my sleep, and I always tell people that's how I practice my speech skills. That night, he once again didn't sleep well because I sleepwalked to his bed. Robert, who was hearing and didn't know I was a sleepwalker, opened his eyes and was terrified to find me hovering over him. The moment he realized that I was getting ready to choke him, he was about to scream like a little boy. Luckily, I woke up just as my hands touched his neck. I quickly backed off and scooted back to bed as if nothing had happened. He could hardly go back to sleep, he was so scared—understandably so.

As usual, I loved to make people laugh. Here, I mimic Clarke Treasurer Ed Hubbard, who often spoke with a cigarette hanging out of his mouth, making it difficult to lipread him.

Always the practical joker, I was constantly putting somebody on the spot, but always in good spirits. Sometimes, during staff meetings, I crossed my eyes and made faces at the interpreters until they cracked, much to their chagrin. Often, when I joked with hearing people in conversations, they couldn't tell if I was joking or had merely misunderstood what they said. There would be an uncomfortable pause as they tried to figure out if I was joking or not, since I would often keep a straight face—magnifying the effectiveness of my jokes. Sometimes I would tell the staff how much I enjoyed the music in the room, and they'd express their delight. Of course I didn't enjoy the music!

I also served as a dorm director for sixty Upper School boys and girls at Bell Hall and Yale House for two years. Although there were TTYs on each floor, most of the houseparents had no idea of how to use them. So I spent a lot of time on foot talking with the house parents and students. Even the houseparents often came to my family quarters to ask for assistance with students—as often as every hour. Soon, I got fed up with their constant requests, so I began to answer the door naked, except for a towel around my waist. The first time they saw me in this attire, they were visibly shocked, and immediately averted their eyes. It worked; they rarely came to my door after that.

Since the students knew I was deaf, they would try to get away with saying things behind my back, either in a class or at the dorm, but they forgot that I had two eyes in front and two on the back of my head! I had been around for a long time, and I knew all about their tricks. They often marveled at how quickly I caught them, even if they were out of my line of sight.

There was one time when one of the school administrators was in the process of moving from Bell Hall to a temporary apartment. She was always reminding the staff to not leave any items or furniture in the hallways anywhere on campus due to fire regulations, yet she had left most of her furniture in the living room. I wasn't too pleased about this, so I wrote down on a piece of paper, "You are welcome to take any furniture. FREE!" and placed it on the furniture. Some people grabbed a few of the items immediately. Of course, the administrator screamed when she found some of her furniture missing. In the end, the furniture was returned.

Since my family and I lived on campus, we needed a place to go to during the holidays and summers. We bought a small cottage in Dennisport in Cape Cod in 1980. In the summer of 1982, Linda was pregnant again, and her water broke while walking on the beach. I immediately took her to Cape Cod Hospital. At 12:30 a.m. on July 11, Keith Robert was born two weeks early at eight pounds and two ounces. Like with Kevin Jr., we couldn't make up our minds about his name. The nurse told us we couldn't take him home without a name, or otherwise she would name the baby "Danny." So we hurriedly named him Keith Robert. Even though Keith had been an unexpected pregnancy, we were delighted to have a new addition to the family. When the doctor came, he had a hard time breaking the news that Keith was deaf. I quickly responded with a big smile, "Oh, don't worry about it! I'm ready to take him home!" The doctor was perplexed, since most people didn't have such a positive reaction.

The Lower School kids often asked me about my bald head (the toupee I wore during college was happily thrown away after graduation). So I always told them my story. "One day in Cape Cod, I was mowing the lawn and it was such a hot day. I got tired and decided to take a break. I took a catnap right on the grass. Not realizing that the lawn mower wasn't shut off, my son Keith, who was three at the time, pushed it and accidentally ran it over my head. My hair was all gone! My head was bleeding! I was rushed to the hospital and had to have stitches!" I would then show the students my head and ask them to look for the scars. Poor Keith! His friends always went over to him and expressed their horror. "How could you do that? Hurting your own daddy? Bad boy!" Even the parents came up to me asking if the story their child had told them was true. Poor parents!

Every time someone asked me about my family, I shared that my wife and three children were deaf. They naturally were surprised, since most of them had never been exposed to or met a deaf family before. I would then mention that we had a deaf dog… and a deaf bird, too. Their eyes always got bigger and bigger at every mention of another deaf member of the family, and their mouths would be wide open in awe. I didn't stop there; I'd add that I also had deaf fish. At this point, some people would realize I was pulling their legs, but others wouldn't. Of course, I didn't let them know I was kidding. Why would I? My deadpan face was my best asset.

When Gawith Hall was under renovation, I quietly shared with the teachers and houseparents, among other staff, that the construction workers had found a skeleton in the basement. It was possible that the skeleton belonged to one of the workers who died or was murdered while building the hall back in 1870. "FBI agents are on the way to investigate it," I informed the staff members. Their faces registered shock and horror, but then they remembered my usual tricks and told me they knew I was joking. Straight-faced, I insisted I wasn't, and showed them pictures of me wearing a hat and raincoat (with my face obscured), examining a skeleton in the basement tunnel of Gawith Hall. (Shh! I borrowed the skeleton from the science classroom and staged the whole photo.) Their faces transformed back to expressions of panic.

"I can't believe I slept in the same building with a dead body in the basement!" they screamed at me. It was a sobering day at Clarke, with people upset and in disbelief. Some came up to me and asked if it was true about the dead body, and I looked down, nodding sadly, and walked away as if I didn't want to discuss it anymore. One of the houseparents admitted she could hardly sleep for a few days. Even the two alumni members on the Clarke school board could not believe it when I shared the tragic news immediately before their regular board meeting. Like the others, they at first did not take me seriously, but then when they saw the photos, they realized it was serious. They questioned themselves, "Why didn't President Gjerdingen share this with us? Why didn't he report the discovery of the skeleton to the board?" Once they asked President Gjerdingen, they found out that it was only another elaborate hoax on my part, and were ready to kill me! Fortunately, I didn't get in trouble.

Visiting Scholar in Texas

In 1988, Dr. Wallace Bruce, a former Clarke employee, invited me to teach at the Sunshine Cottage School for Deaf Children, an oral school in San Antonio, Texas. Like Clarke, Sunshine Cottage had a policy that did not allow the school to hire deaf people. Even so, Dr. Bruce wanted to show the school board how important it was for the school to have deaf role models, and convinced the board to bring me in for one year. I took a leave of absence from Clarke and brought the whole family to San Antonio. It proved to be a rewarding and fun year for the family, and I like to think that the Sunshine Cottage also benefited from my presence.

I was invited back for another year, but I decided to return to Clarke. The Sunshine Cottage did hire some deaf teachers after I left, certainly a step in the right direction.

Retirement

Just before I retired from Clarke, one of the administrators' secretaries wasn't in a good mood. She came to my office a couple of times asking for my end-of-the-year report. She grew tired of running after me, but finally I was ready to submit the report. I asked her if she wished to have my disk with the file, and the secretary became visibly shocked and upset. She walked out of the office immediately without saying a word. I was puzzled and tried to figure out what had happened. For two weeks, I noticed some staff members looking at me as if they were shocked at my behavior, but I could not figure it out and decided to let it go. Finally, Michael O'Connell came to my office and sat down. He pointed at the disk, which was right next to the computer and asked what it was. I wondered why he was asking such a dumb question and I spoke, "Disk." With a smile, Michael replied, "Well, Kevin, do you remember when the secretary came over to your office asking for your report? She thought you asked her if she wanted your 'dick!'" I burst out laughing and still chuckle today at that experience.

I ended my fifty-year association with Clarke School as a student, parent, and staff member in 2000. By then, my family had moved to Maryland.

CHAPTER 9

Getting My Foot in the Door

This picture appeared in the Daily Hampshire Gazette on February 5, 1985. The caption read, "Hearing-impaired juror Kevin John Nolan, foreground, watches the lips of Lauri Krouse, an interpreter hired by the state to repeat what is being said in the courtroom for Nolan."

On a cold January 3, 1985, a deputy sheriff came to Yale House at Clarke and handed me a summons to jury duty. I went to the Hampshire County Courthouse and notified Court Clerk Norma June Thibodo of my interest. Norma June, who had served as the county clerk for twenty-three years, upon learning I was deaf, reassured me I would be waived from jury duty. Unlike most people thrilled to not have to perform this duty, I was taken aback, because I strongly believed it was my constitutional right and civic duty to serve. I asked her why, and this seemed to catch her off guard. She said she didn't know, but I pressed on, wanting a clear reason. This forced her to check with the office of the Superior Court and other legal offices to make sure there was no law prohibiting a deaf citizen from serving. Indeed, there was nothing in the law precluding deaf people.

The jury summons I received in 1985.

As number eighteen among seventy-five jurors in that month's jury pool, I became the first deaf citizen in Hampshire County history to serve on a jury; the case was a drunk driving case. With a state-hired oral interpreter sitting in front of the jury box and silently repeating everything spoken, I sat ready to serve. However, the defendant failed to appear, so I never got to hear the case.

This experience sparked a fire in me, and I now realized it was my obligation to teach people about deaf people's capabilities, as well as to overcome misconceptions. I also wanted the Northampton community to be aware of the communication services available, such as the TTY, relay services, interpreting services, and more, in public places such as the library, fire and police departments, city offices, schools, and hospitals. To get my foot in the door, I wrote a letter to Mayor David Musante expressing my interest in serving as a member of the city's handicapped (this term was later changed to "disabled") committee. Mayor Musante's response was positive, and I was appointed to the committee. This gave me the opportunity to learn how the city worked and also to meet public officials and residents. Meanwhile, I continued to be active in the deaf community, pushing state bills to form the Office of Deafness (later Massachusetts Commission for the Deaf and Hard of Hearing), state-funded relay services, interpreting services, and many other issues. I was fortunate to work with pioneering deaf advocates such as Dr. Richard Thompson, Barbara Jean "BJ" Woods, Ruth Moore, and Jack Levesque. I was also involved with various organizations such as the Clarke Alumni Association, DEAF, Inc., Hampshire County United Way campaigns, Alexander Graham Bell Association for the Deaf, and National Commission on Equal Educational Opportunities for Deaf Children as appointed by Chairperson Roslyn "Roz" Rosen (who would later become the Director of the National Center on Deafness at California State University, Northridge). My involvement and work with each organization built my confidence in becoming more active with the city and proving that deaf citizens could knock down the barricades that traditionally kept us out of politics.

In 1983, I attended a city council meeting for the first time, but found it difficult to follow the discussions and proceedings since there was no interpreter. The next day I went to the city hall and asked the mayor's administrative assistant, Marcia Burick, for help finding funds for interpreting. Fortunately for me, Ms. Burick was also part of the Handicapped committee, so we became immediate allies in this project. She wrote a request to the city council asking for $500. At the next city council meeting, the request was discussed, and Councilor James Brooks suggested that citizens requesting this service who could afford to pay for the interpreters should be asked to do so. I was displeased with his comments and was about to get up and sarcastically say that Brooks and the councilors should pay the city clerk for taking meeting notes. Before I could so, Ms. Burick reminded Councilor Brooks that interpreting services were mandated by Section 504 of the Rehabilitation Act of 1973 and were to be available to everyone at no charge. Councilor Brooks withdrew his statement, and the council approved $522 for interpreting services requested in advance. This was a small, but important, victory for the deaf community.

Interestingly, thirty-five years after my first jury duty experience, I received a summons to go to the Palm Beach

County Courthouse in Florida for jury duty. When I arrived at the courthouse, they had an interpreter ready for me. It was amazing to see how much has changed, and I was delighted to be able to simply walk in and begin my civic duty.

CHAPTER 10

Throwing My Hat into the Ring

I was at my office desk when I decided to run for City Council.

One of the greatest constitutional rights of every American, hearing or deaf, is to run for public office. It is an integral component of America democracy—yet deaf people often are not part of this process for a number of reasons, primarily oppression and disempowerment. Renowned Deaf historian Jack Gannon found during his research for Deaf Heritage that there hadn't been any born-deaf politician at that point (there was a deaf man, John W. Michaels, of Goshen, Virginia, who served a four-year term as city councilor—but he had become deaf at the age of eight).

I had always loved politics with a passion ever since the Kennedy era. My interest in politics was mostly inspired by Clarke civics teacher Mrs. Violet Pratt. Every morning at breakfast, I would talk with my teachers about news throughout the world and politics. I had tried talking with my friends, but they had no interest in politics—so I went over to the adults instead.

I always wanted to experience campaigning and meeting constituents face-to-face while discussing their issues. As a citizen, I had long wanted to serve constituents, but never took steps to actually run for office because I worried how people would react upon learning I was deaf. I began to talk with people about the possibility of running for office, and was bombarded with many reasons on why I should not run. "How? You are deaf. It's impossible!" they would say. Although it was difficult overcoming such negativity, I was compelled by my passion for politics to give it a try.

Adding to the challenge was the fact that I was relatively unknown among the community outside of my circle of friends. My ward, Ward 2 (the same one Calvin Coolidge represented eighty-seven years before), had an incumbent running for reelection. William Ames was a well-respected Republican who had served on the council for twenty years with a reputation for integrity. He was also a Northampton native. Defeating Ames would require a lot of hard work, and many tough steps. I asked myself questions to determine if I was ready to run or not, such as:

- "Am I willing to accept the sense of isolation and loneliness that candidates and office holders sometimes feel?"
- "Do I have the time to run for and hold public office?"
- "Can I accept the anger or criticism of voters if I make a decision contrary to their opinion?"
- "Am I able to function with all kinds of people?"
- "Am I able to control my emotions?"
- "Will the voters accept me as a person?"
- "Are they willing to communicate with me?"
- "Do I have broad-based support for my candidacy?"

- "Can I promote myself?"
- "Will I accept negative reactions?"
- "Do I have plenty of stamina and energy for the tasks I have to do?"

As I mulled over the answers to these questions, I remembered the advice I always gave my students: "Don't let being deaf stop you. Try it and go for it. You will be respected whether you succeed or fail." I also kept thinking about how I always said, "Keep trying, or you'll regret it for the rest of your life." I needed to practice what I preached.

After some time, I ultimately took my own advice and decided to run for office.

CHAPTER 11
Taking the First Steps

I ran in Northampton Ward 2, the same ward that U.S. President Calvin Coolidge campaigned for 87 years earlier.

On July 2, 1985, I went to Northampton City Hall and asked City Clerk Adeline Murray for the paperwork to seek nomination for the Ward 2 city council seat. Armed with the forms, I returned home and asked Linda to be the first to sign the nomination paper. Despite her initial reservations about the long hours I might be away from our family, especially since I was still working at Clarke at this point, she signed it with full support.

The form required signatures of at least 100 registered voters, so I went door-to-door in the Ward 2 neighborhood to collect signatures. My first break came from within the family: Kevin, Jr. was a newspaper boy delivering the Daily Hampshire Gazette, one of the oldest newspapers in the United States. As a result of Kevin Jr.'s paper route, he had made many new friends along his route—which proved to be a valuable asset for my efforts to get the required signatures.

The minimum number was met without difficulty.

Nine days later, at 11:00 a.m. on July 11—which also happened to be my youngest son Keith's third birthday—I stood in the very same classroom at Clarke School where I had started my schooling thirty-five years before. The room was filled with

The family in 1985 during my campaign. L-R: Kristi Ann, Kevin Jr., Linda, me, and Keith.

my family, Kevin's first teacher Marcia (Ackely) Langdon, other teachers, staff, and administrators, and a reporter from the Daily Hampshire Gazette. Expressions of surprise went through the audience as I announced my plans to run as a Democrat for the Ward 2 City Council seat, but the surprise quickly turned to full-fledged support. "If Kevin's from Massachusetts, then politics is in his blood," they said. They knew I would give the incumbent, William Ames, a good fight, even if it would be a hard fight. After all, Councilor Ames was more experienced, and had run unopposed in past elections. Exacerbating the challenge was that, even though I had attended Clarke for thirteen years, I wasn't a Northampton native. After coming back from Rochester, I had lived in the city for only six years, and was unknown to most residents.

Building Support

With the campaign officially launched, I got busy putting together my campaign committee. I first appointed Clarke Speech Coordinator Pat Archambault (later Blinn) as campaign manager. She was a long-time Democrat and chairperson of the city's Handicapped Committee

that I served on.
The campaign
committee
consisted of
six additional
members: Peter
Jones as treasurer,
Stanford Blish,
brothers George
and Bob Sears,
Marcia Langdon,
and Nancy Sheehan.
We decided that the
campaign slogan
would be, "It's time
for a change!" My

My campaign team included (back row, L-R) Dan Cronin, Bob Cahillane, Peter Jones, George Sears, Nancy Sheehan, (front row) Bob Sears, me, and Pat Blinn.

platform emphasized the need for new thinking on the issues that confronted the city. I also pointed out that Northampton, with a population of 30,000, had seen enough business development and should work for more public services, and encourage construction of lower-priced homes. I stressed that I would work to improve education in the city schools, and that city employees and residents should be addressed before the council discussed their concerns and agenda.

After I announced my candidacy, the campaign picked up speed and attracted considerable attention at the local and state levels. Several key Democrats endorsed me. For instance, among Kevin Jr.'s newspaper customers were the Sears family, well-known lifelong residents of Northampton. They launched one of the biggest drives to help secure votes for me. Brothers George and Bob Sears introduced me to State Representative William Nagle, who immediately became another enthusiastic supporter. Mayor Musante referred me to his own reelection committee, which provided me with strong support. Another key Northampton resident, car dealer Robert Callihane, the son of former mayor James Callihane who held office from 1953 to 1959, became a staunch supporter and a valuable campaign worker. So did

Daniel Cronin, circulation manager of the Daily Hampshire Gazette; he had been a basketball referee at Clarke during my school years. Attorney Edward M. O'Brien, a member of the Governor's Council, Tom Hennessey from WHMP radio station, and former Northampton policeman and real estate developer Richard Shea, were among my biggest supporters.

Quickly becoming my right-hand man was Rodney Kunath, a long-time friend and Clarke alumnus. He was known in the community for his Reddy 1954 Chevrolet, and knew almost everyone in town. Kunath had such a love for Northampton and believed in my campaign so much that he purchased a house in the Ward 2 district and registered to vote just a couple of weeks before the deadline. He was sometimes called the honorary mayor of Northampton because of his dedication to the city.

The campaign's start-up strength came largely from high-visibility supporters such as former Mayor Wallace Puchalski's wife Shirley, Councilors Raymond LaBarge, John Fitzgerald, Ed Keefe, Joan Kochin, Leonard Budgar, and Ward 4 candidate Mike Ahearn.

Lingering Resistance

Despite such outstanding endorsements, a number of residents were unwilling to support me because of my lack of political experience, and concerns about being able to communicate with or contact me. Relay services existed by then, but they were largely ineffective. Even the TTY was ineffective in terms of time and ease. I had to figure out a strategy, and quickly.

CHAPTER 12

Going into Full Campaign Mode

I spent a lot of time campaigning by going to people's houses and having one-on-one conversations with them.

Between July and September at our summer home on the Cape, I spent a lot of time planning, making posters and signs, writing speeches, and asking for contributions. To convince my constituents that I had the capacity to serve them well, I decided to embark on a door-to-door campaign strategy. With Linda's help, I knocked on almost every door in Ward 2 (which had a population of 4,000) in all kinds of weather for two months before the election on November 3. I talked, and talked, and talked with people about issues and provided new ideas in response to old problems. I actually felt like a parrot at times because I repeated the same message to every constituent.

The deaf community expressed a strong desire to see me communicate in sign language rather than speaking only. I didn't sign during my campaign mainly because I knew once I signed, I would likely push voters away based on their misconceptions and doubts about deaf people. Even though we had made great strides

I read the newspaper daily to keep up with local politics. See the holes in my shoes? They came from walking so much as I knocked on hundreds of doors during the campaign.

in awareness about deaf people, misconceptions still were widespread. The famed Deaf President Now protest hadn't taken place yet at Gallaudet; the Americans with Disabilities Act hadn't yet been enacted; and people were still struggling to accept that sign language, as proven by researchers, was a language distinct from English.

Interestingly enough, throughout the campaign, people never asked about my being deaf. Maybe they just wanted to show their respect and avoid offending me. Sure, some constituents were unwilling to talk to me, but never let on if it was because of their disinterest in politics, because they had no patience to listen, or were uncomfortable about talking to a deaf man. One person did say he wouldn't vote for me because he didn't want his taxes spent on interpreting services. Despite people's resistance to politics in general, I played upon one of my greatest assets: my sense of humor. I found that humor helped put people at ease. It certainly was not an easy task, but it was a most challenging and worthwhile one. I quickly learned the essential traits of a successful candidate: large doses of tolerance, patience, light humor, open-mindedness, and persistence.

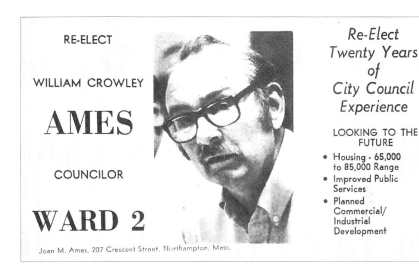

My opponent's and my campaign flyers.

The Northampton Democratic Committee and League of Women Voters hosted my debates with opponent Bill Ames. The debates became crucial components of my campaign because they gave me the opportunity to convince voters of my capacity to answer to them and serve them effectively— and I did so well that I gained supporters after each one. The radio was a thorn in my side, though; most candidates used this to campaign, including Bill Ames. To get around this obstacle, I asked several supporters to speak for me, although I wasn't too comfortable about this approach. I preferred that people heard my own words in my own voice.

Clarke students in government classes also became involved with my campaign; I deeply believed it would be a great educational experience for them. They spent a lot of time holding signs and handing out flyers through Election Day. I knew the sight of deaf children's involvement would have an impact upon voters. Also, it was an important aspect of the campaign that deaf children see deaf adults succeeding in such an important event like a political campaign. Although the response was overwhelmingly positive, one person did call the school to complain because he thought it was a conflict of interest that the students were using school vans.

Meanwhile the Republican opponent, Bill Ames, didn't do much campaigning, instead allowing his distinguished record of twenty years' experience to speak for itself. Unlike me, Ames didn't even place signs on lawns around the district. The one time he did use a campaign sign was a small one on Election Day. I wasn't worried, though; I was completely focused on my own campaign. As months passed, more and more people began supporting me, and the mood shifted. Our campaign team began to realize that a win was more than possible, and became more determined than ever.

CHAPTER 13
Election Day

Election Day was a rainy day, but that didn't dampen our spirits. Clarke brought students and teachers in a van that had signs attached, as seen here.

The morning of November 5, 1985—Election Day— brought a cold, steady rain. The foothills of Mt. Holyoke and Mt. Tom had given up their breathtaking colors to the impending New England winter. While taking a shower, I said to myself, "Well, no matter if I win or lose, I'll feel good because I did my best." I was slightly concerned that the weather would affect voter turnout, with people choosing to stay inside where it was dry and warm. My family, including my mother-in-law Stella, and I arrived at 10:00 a.m. at the Ward 2 polling area, held at Smith Vocational School. Some Clarke students and teachers showed up to hold campaign signs for the day; the Clarke school van had a big sign in red, white, and blue that proclaimed, "Time for a Change" attached to it.

Despite the steady rain, I stood outside greeting voters. A deaf man who I knew somewhat was hanging around the polling place, both inside and outside, with a big sign begging people to vote for me. This was against the state regulations; people were allowed to carry signs only if 100 feet away from the polling place. This man was asked to leave, but he refused. I was very concerned because this man could cost me votes, so I asked my right-hand man to help. Rod went after him and physically dragged him to a spot where he could hold his sign. I was relieved that he stayed there with no trouble.

The campaign was a family affair. Top: My mother-in-law Stella Howe, Kristi Ann, Keith, and Linda helped on Election Day. Bottom: Kevin Jr.

Three people gave me their umbrellas, and I stayed until the polls closed at 8:00 p.m. Bill Ames didn't arrive till later in the afternoon with a small sign, and only a handful of his volunteers were there. Bill and I joked with each other while greeting voters. It was clear that Bill was fully confident he would be reelected.

Normally, a cold rainy day would hamper voter turnout, but the city of Northampton took its politics seriously. That day, a record of number of votes were cast, mostly after work,

With my opponent William "Bill" Ames and his small campaign sign on Election Day.

making it one of the longest days in my life. When the polls finally closed at 8:00 p.m., the tallying of votes began. This took what seemed to be endless hours because each paper ballot had to be counted by hand. Linda and I went from one table to another as if waiting for our baby's birth. My team later told me that it was at this point they noticed how the ballot counters started to whisper to each other in apparent surprise, but I was beyond exhausted and

The election ballot.

didn't notice anything at the time. Later in the evening, Bill Ames and his son came in expressing their concerns about possibly losing. I began to realize how differently people were behaving, with one vote counter dropping hints that I had a good number of votes. This made me extremely nervous, especially not knowing what to expect or what to do next. But only the city clerk could officially announce the results.

Just after midnight, Linda and I walked into the crowded Northampton City Hall. Everything happened so fast, it was almost all a blur. The news

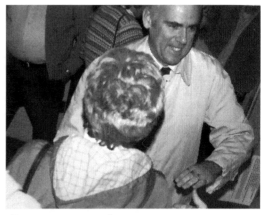

So many people came up to congratulate me on the victory that everything was a blur.

arrived that I had just upset an immensely popular veteran councilor in the race. People erupted in cheers, and Mayor Musante, State Representative Bill Nagle, Jr., and some councilors greeted me with slaps on my back, hugs, and hearty handshakes. Overwhelmed at the support, I was immediately escorted to another room for an unexpected interview with Joe Fennessey of Northampton's radio station, WHMP, and I could see other reporters clamoring to get interviews with me. Although I had no interpreter with me, I did the best I could. After the brief radio talk, I went to see City Clerk Murray to officially receive the final results. With a big smile, she congratulated me. By then, it was well past midnight, and she announced that I had won by a razor-thin margin of seven votes. I was numb and kept saying, "I can't believe I won!" Ames, visibly upset, came to me and politely congratulated me, but then left quickly. For the next hour or so, I spent time talking with well-wishers and reporters. At 1:30 a.m., with the votes finally tallied and all parties satisfied with the "lucky seven" votes, Linda, Rodney Kunath, and I went out for a victory breakfast of cheeseburgers at a diner.

Meanwhile, Linda's friends were teasing her, telling her to get ready to move into the White House in a few years. This was the same city that sent Calvin Coolidge from Ward 2 up the political ladder to the presidency. After that historical night, an inspired Kevin Jr. asked me, "Can I run against you 20 years from now?" I heartily replied, "Absolutely! You can even use the same slogan: It's time for a change!"

I was now the first deaf city councilor in the United States. But first, I had a surprise for my family.

CHAPTER 14

Rubbing Elbows with Royalty

Four days after being elected, I took my family to meet Princess Diana, who Kristi Ann (left) so admired. Keith is next to her.

Throughout Election Day, I had another pressing matter on my mind, one that I couldn't tell anyone about for a few days. I was on the verge of becoming the first born-deaf person to be elected to a public office both in Massachusetts and in the United States, but I also had a surprise I had been planning. I couldn't tell my wife or children, because they would become distracted and I wanted to focus on the election. My big news was that our family had been invited to greet Prince Charles and Princess Diana as they arrived at Washington's Andrews Air Force Base for a whirlwind American tour on November 9, 1985—their first trip as a married couple.

The morning after the election, after coming home from the diner, I broke the news to the family. They were stunned at first, very quiet. The election victory immediately became a thing of the past for the children, especially for seven-year-old Kristi Ann. It was a dream come true for her, a tireless fan of the Princess of Wales. She read everything she could about Princess Diana. A few weeks before, when she heard that Prince Charles and Princess Diana would visit America, she told me she wished to meet Princess Diana. I said, "If you really want to

We visited Congressman Silvio Conte (R, MA) before meeting the British Royal family. In back are Congressman Conte, Linda, and me. In front are Kristi Ann, Keith, and Kevin Jr.

meet her, write a letter to the White House." She took my advice and wrote a letter to the White House. A letter came explaining that the White House was not responsible for their visit; rather, it was the British Embassy's responsibility. So with my help, Kristi Ann wrote a letter to Congressman Silvio O. Conte of Pittsfield, Massachusetts (yes, the same Congressman Conte who was the guest speaker at my graduation ceremony twenty-two years earlier) asking for a special invitation to present flowers to the royal couple.

I later received a call at work from the British Embassy. The secretary interpreted the call, and I learned that we had officially received an invitation to meet the couple. The legwork involved in securing a place on the tarmac for our family was considerable, especially since the invitation had been a last-minute addition.

Operating, barely, on no sleep two days after the election, I drove through the night for eight hours to bring my family to Washington, DC. After a few hours of sleep at a friend's house, we got up early to drive to the city and visit Congressman Conte to express our appreciation for his help in making this happen. Next, we drove to the British Embassy on Massachusetts Avenue to pick up the necessary papers and passes for the big day.

The following day, we drove to the Andrews Air Force Base several miles away from the capital city, and showed our passes to the security people at the gate. For some reason, our paperwork wasn't accepted, and we were told to join the big crowd instead of on the red-carpeted tarmac. We, needless to say, were upset—until a stroke of luck came our way. I spotted the lady who had handed me the papers at the British Embassy standing at the gate. I ran up to her and explained this situation. She quickly took care of matters, and we were allowed to enter, much to our relief—especially Kristi Ann!

What took place next happened so quickly. Kevin Jr. was so nervous that his knees shook as Prince Charles and Princess Diana came out of the plane and walked down the red-carpeted tarmac. Princess Diana walked over to our daughter, and not knowing it was against protocol, the star-struck Kristi Ann hugged her. Kristi Ann then presented a bouquet of red flowers, which coincidentally matched Princess Diana's dress. I told Princess Diana how much Kristi Ann idolized her and how many books she had read about her. Laughing, Princess Diana replied, "Oh, it is a bad education for her." I then spoke to Prince Charles, "We are from Northampton—" Charles interrupted and asked if we were from Northampton, England. Keith, who was only three years old, had no idea what was going on. He seemed to greatly enjoy chewing on the pole of the miniature British flag he was holding.

In addition to the media coverage of the historical election only a few days before, our family's meeting with the royal couple was well-documented in the media. Time, Life, Newsweek, the Boston Herald, the Washington Post and many other publications ran photos and news of our children meeting the royal couple.

CHAPTER 15

My Dream
Faces Uncertainty

Taking the oath on Inauguration Day in January 1986.

A few days later, the defeated Councilor Bill Ames called letting me know that he intended to contact the Massachusetts Secretary of State and request a recount because the margin was too close for his liking, a move that caught me by surprise. Ames said he knew of ten supporters who were out of town on Election Day and if he had gotten absentee ballots to them, he might have had a three-vote margin over me. Even so, he admitted he didn't have an awful lot of hope, because he figured the results were pretty accurate.

What this meant for me was that the official results would have to be held until after a recount on November 30. Adding to my stress was that the Commonwealth of Massachusetts was closely monitoring the recount—meaning I could still lose. Several of my key supporters helped settle my worries by monitoring the recount for me. After a very long few weeks, I began feeling nauseated and sick from the stress of waiting, and wondering if there indeed had been a miscount.

In the City Council chambers, I am standing at far right, next to my opponent William Ames, as Board of Registrars of Voting Clerk Patricia Shaughnessy announces the results of the Ward 2 recount. (Photo courtesy of Daily Hampshire Gazette, Mon., Dec. 2, 1985.)

The Final Results

On November 30, Patricia Shaughnessy, Clerk of the Board of Registrars of Voters, finally announced in the council chamber that the recount upheld my election as Ward 2 City Councilor. In fact, they found three additional votes, bringing my victory up to ten votes, from 504-497 to 506-496. The people, mostly my campaign team and supporters, in the room cheered and broke out in applause. Overwhelmed by the relief, I almost lost my composure, but managed to hold back my tears. Ames came and congratulated me for the second time in a month. He said to a reporter, "Kevin waged a very hard campaign and turned out a lot of people." He also admitted he had mistakenly relied on his long experience and the fact that people knew him. His wife was a bit more emotional, crying as she said she couldn't believe Bill's constituents had turned their backs on him and voted for me.

The rest of the country was swamped with the news of me becoming the first deaf-by-birth person to be elected to public office in the United States. The story was reported by the Associated Press and ran in USA Today, New York Times, Boston Globe, Boston Herald, National Enquirer and other

Celebrating victory with supporter Bob Cahillane after the nail-biting recount.

periodicals around the nation. I received congratulatory wishes from all over, including from President Ronald Reagan, Massachusetts Governor Michael Dukakis (who would later run against President George H.W. Bush in 1988), House Speaker Tip O'Neill, and Senator Edward M. Kennedy.

Numerous invitations poured in from mayors of various cities such as Mayor Tom Bradly of Los Angeles, Mayor Diane Feinstein of San Francisco, Boston Mayor Raymond Flynn, and New York City Mayor Ed Koch to visit. Massachusetts Governor Dukakis also invited me to the State House to be introduced to State House Speaker George Keverian, who in turn would introduce me to the legislature in State Chambers. CNN also interviewed me for a feature story. I was floored by all the attention the victory generated.

Mayor David Musante and other elected councilors welcomed me with open arms. It was likely my sense of humor that helped put people at ease as I talked to them. I strongly believe that I was gregarious to the point that they became confident in my abilities. After the recount, car dealer Bob Callihane (the one whose father had been mayor of Northampton at one time) and his wife hosted a victory party for the campaign workers and supporters; they had been the backbone of our success.

Inauguration Day

Inauguration Day was a family affair. (L-R): Keith, Linda, me, Kevin Jr., Cousin Betsy (Washburn) Zito, Kristi Ann, Aunt Mary (Nolan) Washburn, and Dad "Bob."

Inauguration Day was a bright day with snow on the ground, January 6, 1986, in Northampton. The ceremonies at Northampton High School were well attended by Clarke School students and staff, Northampton citizens, and my extended family. When I saw my father Bob walking down the aisle at the ceremonies to witness my historical oath, I nearly broke down in joy. However, I later learned that Bob had initially been reluctant about attending, but Aunt Mary Washburn persuaded him. My mother had passed away in 1982. Still, it hurt that my brothers and sister never called to congratulate me. Each did send me a Christmas card with a short congratulatory note—but it all seemed uneventful to them.

The inauguration was followed by a luncheon in the Coach Light Room at Hotel Northampton. The main speaker was Massachusetts Lieutenant Governor Evelyn Murphy. After her speech, I walked around thanking supporters and volunteers for their help. The other new council members and I left early for our first council meeting at 2:30 p.m.

Mayor Musante got down to business quickly, with Robert Storm, a long time teacher at Clarke, serving as an oral interpreter for me (and the city paid for the interpreters!). First on the agenda was to elect the new council president, Raymond LaBarge. Although the president typically sat across

104

from the mayor, LaBarge offered me his seat so I could follow the councilors on both sides during discussions. Next, we discussed a new parking garage in downtown Northampton. It was during this discussion that I spoke for the first time as a councilor. I stressed the importance of blending the garage into the rest of the downtown's nineteenth century architecture.

Ten days later on January 16, I decided to call my father to let him know of an article in USA Today. When my mother-in-law Stella Howe, who was helping make the call, said that Bob wasn't answering, I asked Aunt Mary to check on him. She agreed, and while waiting for her to call back, I attended the second council meeting. When I went home, I found Stella standing in front of Yale House where we lived. She told me that the school assistant president, Bill Blevins, needed to see me. Suspecting nothing, I went to Bill's residence, and was asked to sit down in the living room. Bill began by saying that Aunt Mary had called. Before he could continue, I had a sinking feeling. I said, "I think I know what you're going to say. He died, right?" When Bill nodded, I immediately thought of how grateful I was that Bob had made it to my inauguration. Bob had died of a massive heart attack at the age of 67.

A few days after Bob's funeral, I attended the Inaugural Ball at Clarion Hotel; Linda was ill with the flu and could not attend. It was a grand event, but a bittersweet one with all the sudden changes in my life.

CHAPTER 16
Life as a Councilor

Speaker of the House Tip O'Neill is shown here breaking the tragic news about the explosion of the space shuttle Challenger.

With so much media attention, I was overwhelmed with invitations and requests from all over. Congressman Conte invited my interpreter (Bill Blevins) and me as his guests to President Reagan's State of the Union address. In Conte's letter, he said he appreciated the efforts of people like me who wish to contribute to the continuous, effective operation of the nation's political system. I had hoped to meet President Reagan since we had a lot in common. I knew President Reagan was a fan of Calvin Coolidge, and I cherished my ties to Calvin Coolidge by way of Ward 2. Both Reagan and I were actors, although at different levels. We both loved jelly beans. And finally, Reagan had hearing loss as did I. The only difference was that Reagan was a Republican, and I was a Democrat.

While in the area, I was scheduled to meet with House Speaker Thomas "Tip" O'Neill, U.S. Senators Edward M. Kennedy and John Kerry (both of whom would later run for president), all from Massachusetts. As I walked into the office of House Speaker Tip O'Neill that morning, I was beaming with excitement; this would be the highlight of my day-long tour. But O'Neill, who solemnly stood to greet me, kept one eye fixed on his television. After shaking hands, O'Neill explained there had been a terrible accident, and that "It blew up. Of course, you knew that." Bill Blevins (my interpreter), Bob Cahillane, and I were perplexed and said we didn't know what was going on. O'Neill sat on his desktop, pointed to a color television set, and said, "Well, look, the space shuttle blew up. Yeah, watch it. I thought you knew about it." It was January 26, 1986. The Challenger had blown up 73 seconds into its flight, killing all astronauts on board. We watched in silence as debris from the Challenger, by then a mere billowing cloud of white smoke against the clear blue sky, fell to the earth. O'Neill told us again, "Watch it," as the television replayed the explosion repeatedly. I quickly thought about Christia McAuliffe, the smiling teacher from New Hampshire who had been selected over hundreds of others for this trip.

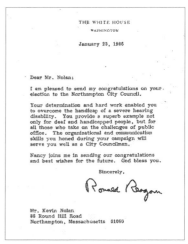

I received a congratulatory letter from U.S. President Ronald Reagan.

Clearly, the explosion brought an abrupt change in mood to what was to have been a glorious visit to the nation's capitol. I felt sick, as did everyone else. The mood at the Capitol had suddenly turned somber. All of the invitations I had accepted were postponed. Despite the tragic overtones, O'Neill and I continued with our meeting. After O'Neill congratulated me on my victory and said, "That's positively beautiful. That's great. That is beautiful. I am honored to have you come in," I returned the compliments by sharing that I had admired his long-time service to Massachusetts and the nation. The burly, white-haired House Speaker responded by wrapping his arms around me and saying, "You make an old man's heart feel good."

I was honored to meet Senator Ted Kennedy, who wished me the best in my new position. At far left is Bob Cahillane; interpreter Bill Blevins is at far right.

I then went to the Russell Senate Office Building and met Senator Kennedy. His office walls were full of pictures and mementos. He praised my triumphant election and noted his son, Teddy, Jr., was waging a campaign to promote the achievements

Just before President Reagan's State of Union speech, I met Senator Robert Dole and Secretary of Transportation Elizabeth Dole. Next to me is interpreter Bill Blevins.

of people with disabilities. He said, "I am always reminded by my son, Teddy, who lost a leg to cancer, that we're really one accident away from being physically challenged." After visiting Senator Kennedy and exhausted and saddened by the unimaginable Challenger explosion, I flew back to Northampton that evening because the State of the Union address had been rescheduled. ABC's "Good Morning, America" had also invited me for an interview the next morning, but had to cancel it due to the shuttle explosion.

A month later, on February 5, my interpreter and I flew back to the Capitol and took our visitor seats in the U.S. House of Representatives section. I got a

We also met with Massachusetts Governor Michael Dukakis, who went on to run for the presidency of the United States in 1988. (L-R): Brothers Bob and George Sears, Massachusetts State Representative Bill Nagle, Governor Dukakis, Linda, and me.

firsthand look at President Reagan in action as he delivered the State of the Union address. I also met and chatted with Senator Robert Dole of Kansas and his wife, Elizabeth H. Dole, Secretary of Transportation, and Madeline Will, Assistant Secretary for Special Education and Rehabilitative Service. This visit was rewarding, and I saw firsthand the work involved and influence politicians had that affected Americans on a daily basis.

Later that spring, I attended a White House reception marking the tenth anniversary of P.L. 94-142, the Education for All Handicapped Children Act (now the Individuals with Disabilities Education Act, or IDEA). This law guaranteed children with disabilities the right to a free, appropriate education in a least restrictive setting. Both First Lady Nancy Reagan and Madeline Will, Assistant Secretary for Special Education at the U.S. Department of Education, gave talks.

CHAPTER 17
Getting Back to Business

The 1986-1988 Northampton City Council. (Back, L-R): James Brooks, Edward Keefe, me, Paul Bixby, Raymond LaBarge, and Michael Ahern. (Front, L-R): John Fitzgerald, Joan Kochin, Mayor David Musante, and Leonard Budgar.

Serving on the Northampton Council wasn't easy. I also had a full-time job at Clarke, which meant I became adept at juggling commitments. I attended countless subcommittee and council meetings for two years. Mayor Musante appointed me to three committees: Fire, Ordinance, and Claims. Reaching my constituents was at times difficult due to the lack of relay services. The only, and best, way to communicate was to visit in person. Although this was effective, it was also time-consuming. The city paid each councilor a stipend of $500 per year, which I went through quickly because of the extra time I had to take to visit people.

There were many steps in place that helped me do my job better. For example, Council President Ray LaBarge usually came to my office at Clarke to share city news and updates on

111

issues of concern to the council. This was especially useful because I sometimes had trouble following fast and furious council debates, especially since watching the interpreter meant at least a five-second

As I participated in the Northampton City Council meeting, Dan Salvucci interpreted for me.

delay in information—and by the time I tried to speak up, the group had moved onto other topics, or called on other people. I usually had to ignore the interpreter to watch the speaker directly to ensure I could speak up before others. I sometimes quietly mouthed words to indicate my reactions or opinions to my fellow councilors. Even so, I was grateful for the interpreters who worked with me, especially at the last minute. This is especially true for Dan Salvucci, who gave many long hours to ensuring I had communication access.

Meetings were not without drama. Councilor Joan Kochin would yell at me, holding up a sign saying "Read my lips," if I misunderstood or missed her points. Every time I disagreed with Councilor Jack Fitzgerald's opinions or votes, Jack would run to my wife Linda and complain. Funny thing, Linda— then a Republican—would sometimes stand with him, a Democrat himself, instead of me, her husband!

Remember how I always joked or played pranks? That didn't change, of course! Once in a while during a boring meeting, I'd get the attention of some councilors and the city clerk by making faces or strange expressions, causing them to chuckle. Poor Mayor Musante! He could never figure out why they were snickering, wondering if he had said something inappropriate. But if he ever looked at me for help, I would always look innocent and clueless. After the council meetings, the mayor and councilors often went to a local drinking hole,

Fellow Northampton City Council Joan Kochin and I rode in Rodney Kunath's 1954 Chevrolet Bel Air convertible, "Reddy," during the St. Patrick's Day Parade in Boston.

but I rarely joined them because it was often too dark to follow their conversations. That, and my eyes were exhausted from the hard work of trying to keep up with everything during the meetings.

During my term, I helped pass ordinances that added streetlights and speed limit signs. I was especially proud of one achievement. Mayor Musante requested that the city be revitalized to improve the image of downtown Northampton, but he had a small problem with a property owner. The property was a barbershop covered in poorly maintained white wood, an eyesore compared to the rest of the downtown buildings. Mayor Musante tried everything in his power to convince the owner to move another location, and sweetened the deal with a $150,000 offer. But the owner was very stubborn, refusing to give it up. During a meeting when the councilors were discussing how to convince the owner, I raised my hand and expressed my concern about taking a person's property with force. As someone who often had my rights trampled upon, I felt it was undemocratic to force a citizen to give up a property and that city should respect the barbershop owner's wishes. A few minutes later, the owner showed up at this meeting, expressing his anger and frustration. The Council decided to drop the matter. The owner repeatedly thanked

As a member of the Fire Committee, I helped push for three new fire trucks for the city of Northampton. Fire Chief Jeremiah Driscoll, left, was pleased.

me afterward, which was the best feeling for me.

As a member of the Fire Committee, two other members and I helped obtain state grants to purchase three new fire trucks for the city. Other major issues I was involved with included the Northampton Parking Garage, high school renovations, racism, Greenbelt Walkway, Hotel Northampton preservations, and a skateboard park. Before I cast any vote, however, I always talked with my constituents to ask for their opinions. It was important for me to have close contact with them so that I could represent them accurately.

One time some councilors and I were asked to take a look at the shooting range in the basement of Northampton Police Department, so we could decide whether to appropriate money for improvements such as air ventilation. While there, the councilors were asked if they wished to do some shooting. I volunteered, and learned how to hold a gun. As I was about to shoot, Councilor Ed O'Keefe heedlessly tapped my shoulder to talk to me. Startled, I turned around with the gun still in my hand, pointed straight at Ed's face. The group all froze to my puzzlement. A few seconds later, I suddenly realized where the gun was pointed, and hastily put it down. After things calmed down, I continued learning how to shoot.

One issue that I had to deal with was the media. I was always concerned with what was printed in the paper, or said on the news. Despite repeated information for clarification, the reporter still distorted my words or took them out of context, creating problems for the city council or me. Most of the time, I was able to smooth over any misunderstandings. Still, there was one unforgettable incident.

As a city councilor, I took Rodney Kunath to the Massachusetts Democratic Convention in Springfield. Not realizing how enthusiastic Democrat delegates were, I was struck by the importance of having political parties (Democrats and Republicans, for example). One fella named Robert Weiner, a Democrat, had announced earlier he planned to run against the moderate Republican incumbent, Congressman Silvio O. Conte, who had been a major asset to my political career and even family. In almost every election Conte received votes from both Democrats and Republicans. During speeches on the floor, Weiner asked me to sign his nomination form. I was torn, because while I was a Democrat, I was very loyal to Congressman Conte, which Weiner obviously wasn't aware of. I politely declined, but Weiner insisted. I declined again, and walked away hoping Weiner would give up. Not a chance! He kept following me everywhere at the convention, all day long. Irritated, and hoping to get him off my back, I quickly signed his paper, but not before glancing around to make sure nobody was looking.

That following Monday, the Daily Hampshire Gazette made a mention of my endorsement of Weiner. Conte immediately called my friend, Bob Cahillane, and demanded to know why I had signed the paper. I was very upset and embarrassed, and felt terrible. I hadn't intended to betray Conte. I immediately wrote an apology letter to Conte and explained the situation. Much to my relief, Conte understood—but I had learned a hard lesson about media reports and persistence.

CHAPTER 18
Campaigning for a Second Term

SPRINGFIELD REPUBLICAN

In 1987, I ran for re-election on the platform that I still cared about Northampton.

Two years flew by, and it was suddenly time to run for re-election in 1987. Bill Ames announced his intention to reclaim his seat. I knew it was going to be a tough battle because this time Bill wasn't going to take his chances for granted; he was going to fight me to the very end.

I used the same strategy as when I ran in 1985. Many of the supporters from the first campaign returned to help me. Ames, clearly having learned from his mistakes the last time, campaigned heavily from start to end. We both fought hard to the end, and many voters admitted it was difficult for them to decide who to vote for believing that either would do a great job. Ultimately, I lost the re-election by 29 votes. My friends encouraged me to ask for a recount like Ames did back in 1985, but I declined since it was too large of a margin. I was of course disappointed, but took it all in stride. I had done my best, and that was all I could ask for.

Thursday, December 17, 1987 was my last council meeting. It was bittersweet, knowing how much I would miss being a city councilor of Northampton. I would also miss meeting with my constituents, answering their complaints and addressing their grievances at meetings. I also felt as if my political wings had been clipped just as I was ready to fly. During my term, I observed more than I participated, absorbing information and learning the political game. After two years, I was ready to speak up even more, and there was some business I wished to continue working on.

When I was first elected, it was a new challenge for me despite having spent many years fighting so many obstacles such as preconceived notions about my ability to do my job. I believed I had demonstrated to my constituents that I had their best interests at heart, having voted on a wide range of matters on their behalf. Despite being in a fishbowl where everyone was watching me, I had demonstrated that I was willing to sit and discuss issues in people's homes.

I was also proud of the town of Northampton for giving me the opportunity to serve and, most importantly, for becoming a model for other cities that might have hesitated to open their city hall doors to qualified deaf persons ready and willing to serve their fellow citizens. I was extremely appreciative of the mayor, council, city employees and officials, and especially Northampton citizens who treated me as a person, not as someone who was disabled. I was also grateful to the other council members for their patience and cooperation. At the end of my term, the council presented me with a plaque recognizing my contributions to the city, with the mayor saying a few words of praise. The mayor also emphasized that my sense of humor and presence would be missed at meetings. On my way out of the room, I stopped to shake hands with Bill Ames and wished him well.

CHAPTER 19
In the Limelight

Acting has always been a passion, and I was delighted to revive my role as Hardy, this time with Robert Dunn.

Acting has been part of my life ever since I was little. Despite the lack of communication at home, the small black and white television with rabbit ears in the living room was my lifesaver. Without it, I'd probably be in the dark not knowing what was happening in the world. When I was home from Clarke for the holidays, or at school on Saturdays, I would get up each day and watch "Laurel and Hardy" or "The Three Stooges" in the early mornings and "I Love Lucy" in the afternoons. I really loved those shows because of the characters' facial expressions, body movements, and silent mouth movements. I'd imitate the actors for of my family, but they weren't amused. However, when I did the imitations in front of the boys at Clarke during our down time, they would laugh and beg me to do more, even when I exaggerated the stories beyond belief. I loved every minute of it. My first school performances at Clarke were the school's Thanksgiving and Christmas plays. I also was part of several skits as part of the school's speech curriculum. Looking back, I didn't act or express myself effectively because I was more concerned about my speech and pronunciations instead of giving a genuine performance. Still, it helped me in the long run.

In 2008, I returned to my alma mater 40 years after graduating, acting in "Equus" at NTID.

That feeling of exhilaration that came from entertaining people is exactly why I've always loved to act. Even when I was not on stage or in the movies, I still tended to put on a performance in my teaching or public presentations. Those old television shows helped me hone the ability to embody different personalities in my own styles. But acting also provided me with confidence and creativity, especially having grown up in such a sheltered and repressed fashion. I just love that distinct feeling of excitement just before every performance because it really gets my nerves going. It gets me pumping and pushes me to give the best performance I can.

My first experience giving a public presentation in front of a large audience was when I gave the graduation speech at Clarke in June 1963. The audience included all the parents, of course, and guest speaker Congressman Silvio Conte. The sheer irony of this speech is not lost on me: probably none of the students understood what I spoke, given that they would have had to lipread me after watching all the other speakers!

After high school graduation, I didn't have the opportunity to act for a couple of years until I entered NTID. As mentioned, I was an active part of the NTID drama club, and acted alongside famed actors who went on to be part of the acclaimed National Theatre of the Deaf.

After retiring from Clarke, Linda and I flew to Los Angeles in December 2001 to visit our children, Kristi Ann and Keith, at college. We fell in love with California and decided to move to Hollywood. I immediately jumped at the opportunity to act, even if they were minor roles. I played as an extra in films and television shows such as "The Replacements," "Running With Scissors," "Cold Case," and "Sweet Nothing in My Ears" with Academy Award winner Marlee Matlin. I also

I had a doll that looked like me, which I used in my stand-up comedy act, "Who Says Getting Old Is No Fun?"

was privileged to act in "Glee" directed by Julie Dameron, and "A Permanent Grave" directed by Wayne Betts and Chad Taylor and produced by David Kurs (who would go on to become director of Deaf West Theatre).

My prankster antics actually came up during the filming of "A Permanent Grave." The house we were filming in prohibited us from wearing our shoes, and so some twenty pairs of the cast and crew's shoes were on the floor next to the front door in organized rows. During one break from filming, I snuck away and scrambled the shoes. At the end of the long day of filming everyone was more than ready to leave. Imagine their frustration at having to figure out where their shoes were! As I stood there looking innocent, they began bickering and blaming each other. The next day, when they all came back, they continued asking who the culprit behind this prank was, but I never admitted it—until now. Poor souls!

I also acted on stage. I was cast as the villainous Alexander Graham Bell in a play, "Stone Deaf," along with Deaf Studies students at California State University, Northridge. The play was directed by renowned scholars Larry Fleischer, Genie Gertz, and Patrick Boudreault. I also performed a one-man show in Los Angeles and Lake Worth, Florida, "Who Says Getting Old Is No Fun?" In this show, I shared humorous anecdotes about being Deaf senior citizens. I also had a gig acting as Hardy in "The Laurel and Hardy Performance," with my former Clarke student, Rob Dunn. Along with world-renowned deaf comedian John Maucere, we performed on a cruise that had over 4,000 deaf passengers, at Deaf Nation expos, and at several deaf schools.

In 2008, as part of the 40th anniversary of the NTID's founding, I was invited as a member of the college's first class and an original member of the drama club to return to my alma mater's stage. I played the owner of a horse ranch in "Equus," directed by long-time NTID theatre director Jerry Artensinger. It was fun to make new friends and learn from one another, especially with the young cast. I was invited back again in 2018 to take on the role of the Wizard in the "Wonderful World of Oz" play directed by Jim Orr for NTID's 50 year reunion.

After all of those great opportunities and rewarding experiences in Hollywood, Linda and I decided to return to our native Massachusetts.

CHAPTER 20

My Love for the Boston Red Sox

I went to the 2008 Boston Red Sox Fantasy Camp. I had the time of my life, and tried to pretend I couldn't understand the umpire even though I knew exactly what he said.

Despite being a die-hard Red Sox fan, I never wore a Red Sox cap until August of 2004. For some reason, I have always hated wearing caps, not just a baseball cap, but any kind. Even though my family, including my three children (all of whom are big Red Sox fans), always begged me to buy a Red Sox cap every year, I always said "no," because of my dislike for caps.

However, that August was different. Just as I had in the past, I parked at my favorite spot by the Citgo sign to attend a Red Sox/Yankees game, one of the hundreds of games at Fenway that I have attended since my infancy.

While walking down beautiful Yawkey Way, my son, Keith, pulled me to a Red Sox souvenir store and repeated the same request that my children had often made: "Please buy a beautiful blue cap with a bright red B."

As I thought about 59 years of a roller coaster of emotions—including pain, disappointments, broken hearts, and my biggest pet peeve: hearing that same old damn quote, "Wait 'till next year"—I finally decided to buy a cap, hoping it would help break the Curse of the Bambino after 86 fruitless years.

Needless to say, by purchasing this cap, I felt that I contributed to the magic that helped the Red Sox win the World Series Championship! I have to admit that during the American League Championship Series against the Yankees, and the World Series games, I acted like a 10-year old child— screaming, jumping and even closing my eyes on big plays.

I am so proud to be part of this great and memorable team, that to this day I am still wearing this magic cap. This cap will always be treasured as the cap that helped bring a Boston Red Sox World Series Championship to my family and me in our lifetimes.

(Reprinted from www.bostonspastime.com/fans/cap.html)

Fantasy Camp

The idea of going to the Boston Red Sox Fantasy Camp was something I had been toying around with for a while after my retirement. I needed a push to commit, but as the years went by and my body started to give way, that push got much tougher. When the Red Sox team was contesting for the World Series in 2007, I thought it'd be good time for me to register for the 2008 Fantasy Camp in Fort Myers, Florida. At the same time I registered, I requested an interpreter, but it took a while for the Red Sox to decide whether they could meet my request or not. After winning the World Series, the Red Sox office called and offered a spot at the Fantasy Camp free of charge for anyone willing to interpret for me throughout the camp stay. So, I thought of a friend, Roberto Santiago, who was a big Los Angeles Dodgers fan. I asked him, and of course, he grabbed this great opportunity and went with me (little did he know that he would have to sleep in the bathtub due to my loud snoring).

After my arrival at camp in January 2008, we campers, between 30 and 70 years old, were divided into ten teams, and spent a week playing on the team's training fields in teams managed by Red Sox legends new and old. The experience began with a day of tryouts, including batting practice, fielding, base running, and more, leading to a draft and a week of baseball. We campers hadn't even

Hitting the ball off Bill "Spaceman" Lee's pitch.

played ball for such a long time, so after the first day we were all so sore! It was nevertheless a dream come true, filled with a smorgasbord of memories. I had a chance to play with retired Red Sox players such as Jim Rice, Dwight Evans, Carl Yaztremiski, Bill "The Spaceman" Lee, Rich Gedman, Dennis "Oil Can" Boyd, Bob Montgomery, Butch Hobson, Luis Tiant, and Frank Malzone.

After the first day, I was drafted by Butch Hobson, former Red Sox third baseman and manager. My first time at bat in our first game, I singled to left, but as a 62-year-old man, it took me forever to reach first base! I could have hit double! At the end of the game, it was reported that I was the only player with a perfect batting average of 1,000! It only lasted for one day, but oh, yeah, a big deal for me!

During the week's games, "Oil Can" Boyd had a habit of using profanity. So one day I approached him and said, "Boyd, you have a filthy mouth."

Boyd said, "How do you know?"

"Well," I responded, "while playing at the outfield I can read your lips...yes, that far."

Boyd was stunned, and asked, "Really?"

"Yes!" I said.

After that, he turned his back to me so that I could not see his face.

Of course, my inner prankster emerged at baseball camp.

It probably comes as no surprise, but I managed to get in a few of my old tricks. Every time Bob Montgomery, the former Red Sox catcher, made an announcement, I kept cupping my ears, giving him the hint that he needed to speak louder. So, instead of speaking louder, he shouted at all of us. The players made faces, trying to remind Bob that no matter how loud he shouted, I was still deaf.

Another favorite moment for the campers, retired players, and attendees was when I was at bat. From time to time, I would ask the umpire to remove his mask so that I could lipread his calls. It really drove the umpire up the wall.

After the great fun and memorable week, we had a closing banquet and awards were given out to the campers. Considering that I cracked up everyone, I received the "Best Personality" award.

CHAPTER 21
Fighting to Fight

Keith Nolan in his Army ROTC uniform signing "MILITARY."

It seems my love of politics rubbed off on my children, especially Keith, my youngest. Ever since I accompanied my son Keith and his Cub Scouts troop on their overnight stay onboard the USS Massachusetts battleship in Fall River, Massachusetts, and shared information with him about my father's WWII naval service, he was hooked. Keith always wanted to serve in the U.S. military, but under current military standards, deaf and hard of hearing Americans are prohibited from serving in the armed forces. Nevertheless, Keith wanted to try to enlist in the U.S. Navy immediately after he graduated from high school. I took him to the recruiting center in Gaithersburg, Maryland. Unfortunately,

Keith and I walked thousands of steps in Washington, DC to advocate for a military demonstration program.

the navy recruiter's three short words on a scrap of paper derailed Keith's enthusiasm: "bad ear, disqual." That was three months before the 9/11 attacks in 2001.

Undeterred, Keith kept on trying different avenues and branches of the military throughout the years. In 2010, while he worked as a teacher, he asked the Army Reserves Officers' Training Corps (ROTC) at California State University, Northridge, if he could take a few classes with them. They agreed he could, and Keith seized this opportunity to quit his teaching position and then to quickly establish himself as a dedicated, driven participant who took part even in the early-morning workouts and other drills.

When Keith received his military uniform for the ROTC, it was the culmination of all his effort, resiliency and motivation. The instructors recognized his willingness to work hard, train hard, and perform with those at the top of his class. A blow, however, came when he made it through the first and second levels of his training and was beginning to advance to the third. In spite of passing all of the preceding tests, he still needed to pass the one remaining test—the audiology test—before he could move up to the third level. Keith was told he would no longer be able to participate in workouts, drills or trainings. He could audit classes, but he would have to give back his uniform.

With the support of his ROTC cadre, Keith approached Representative Henry Waxman in Los Angeles to successfully request support, and I was

I asked Senator John McCain if he could support Keith's push for a military demonstration program.

proud to accompany him in the many meetings he had. We walked thousands of steps through the Congressional halls of the U.S. Capitol, the Senate buildings of Russell, Dirksen, and Hart, and the House buildings of Cannon, Longworth, and Rayburn. I watched as Keith pushed for his case and gave support in any way I could. We met with legislators such as Senators Tom Harkin (who had a deaf brother), John McCain, Lindsey Graham, and Elizabeth Warren, and Representatives Mark Takano, Henry Waxman, Niki Tsongas, Chris Van Hollen (now Senator), John Delaney, and Jim Langevin.

Sharing many arguments and facts, such as the fact that the U.S. Armed Forces retained many of its service members in Active Duty despite acquiring disabilities during service (hearing loss is the number one disability in the military and the Department of Defense even provides not just hearing aids, but also cochlear implants for some of the service members still in service); the Department of Defense utilizes skills of its deaf and hard of hearing employees and deploys them overseas to work with U.S. military units in military bases; letters of support from various ranks of service members across military branches; and finally the fact that U.S. service members work with deaf Israeli soldiers (the Israel Defense Forces actively accepts deaf Israeli volunteers within their ranks). Keith helped introduce two Congressional

I attended rallies for former U.S. First Lady and the Democratic candidate for the U.S. Presidency Hillary Clinton and for the Republican candidate, Donald Trump, hoping to discuss Keith's cause with them.

bills: S. 1864 and H.R. 5296 during the 113th Congress, which proposed a demonstration program to assess the potential for deaf and hard of hearing Americans to serve in the U.S. Air Force. The House bill was reintroduced as H.R. 1722 during the 114th Congress and was honorably named the Keith Nolan Air Force Deaf Demonstration Act of 2015. Unfortunately, the bills never made it out of the Senate and House Armed Services Committees; hundreds of bills get introduced every year, but only very few are legislated.

Linda and I wrote several letters to President Barack Obama, asking for his assistance, but we never got a response despite having attended his 2012 presidential campaign rally in New Hampshire. This non-response prompted Keith to organize a rally at the North Lawn of the White House on September 12, 2014. Our entire family came to the rally along with some 250 participants from all over the country. We marched from the White House to the U.S. Capitol where there were a series of speakers supporting Keith's case.

When nothing materialized, I attended several senatorial and presidential candidates' campaigns from 2014 to 2016. Luckily, many of the candidates' campaign rallies took place in the state of New Hampshire (since it was the first state to

U.S. Congressman Mark Takano from California has given unwavering support for the demonstration program. He was crucial in providing the House version of the bill.

U.S. Senator Tom Harkin from Iowa, who had a deaf brother, was one of the earliest supporters of Keith and was crucial to introducing the Senate bill for the military demonstration program.

announce partisan candidates in the electoral system), an easy drive over for me from Massachusetts. Senator John McCain was in New Hampshire for Senator Kelly Ayotte's senatorial reelection rally. Inside the Peddler's Daughter pub, I personally spoke with Senator McCain at a table. He nodded and said, "Let me look into it." Incidentally, former senator Scott Brown was also there, and he was already aware of Keith's case since Keith and I had met with him in the fall of 2011. In the long-run though, Senator Kelly Ayotte would prove to be one of

Keith's staunchest supporters; she succeeded in getting language for a feasibility study added to the National Defense Authorization Act of 2016.

I also attended Senator Lindsey Graham's presidential campaign rally in New Hampshire

Senator Kelly Ayotte, shown here with me, was one of Keith's biggest supporters.

where I was able to share a few words with him about Keith's case and give him a letter. Florida Governor Jeb Bush came to New Hampshire and I was fortunate to participate in a town hall forum where he actually called on me. I explained Keith's case and asked whether he'd give his support; he responded that he would need to check with the Department of Defense before deciding anything (there's actually a video of this exchange on YouTube).

When Vice President Joe Biden was in New Hampshire, there were so many people as we pushed to shake his hand. Although I did shake his hand, I was unable to personally talk with him. Nevertheless, I passed on a letter to one of his aides. I went to two of Secretary of State Hillary Clinton's rallies in Florida, but could not get her attention. Donald Trump, who would go on to win the 2016 presidential election, had a town hall meeting in 2015 that I attended in New Hampshire. I kept my hand up in the air, hoping he would call on me, but he didn't. Even so, I spoke with and passed on my letter to his campaign chairman Corey Lewandowski (incidentally, there was a photograph in Newsweek magazine of Trump and me before he took off in his car). I did not hear back from any of these individuals.

Keith's cause took its biggest step forward in May 2018 when the House finally amended the demonstration program provision to their version of National Defense Authorization Act 2019. We were half way through the legislative process! Unfortunately, I was saddened when I learned that the

(L-R): Deaf political advocate Judy C. Stout, U.S. Congressman (now Senator) Chris Van Hollen from Maryland who has given steadfast support for the military demonstration program, Keith, and me.

Senate removed the provision as the bill went through the Conference Committee in July 2018.

While the battle proves to be hard, Keith continues his fight to this day.

CHAPTER 22
Life Goes On

My family in 1992: Keith, Linda, Kevin Jr., Kristi Ann, and me.

I remained involved with the city government for many years, continuing my service on the Handicapped Services Committee. I attended council meetings from time to time to make sure the council would broaden its view by looking beyond the needs of the downtown area to the rest of the city, particularly on issues related to education and racism. I also watched the meetings on local cable at home, which proved to be difficult since they weren't captioned. In 1990, I received a ticket from Congressman Conte, my longtime supporter, to the White House South Lawn to witness President George H.W. Bush sign the historical Americans with Disabilities Act (ADA) in 1990.

Since my election, several deaf individuals have run for public office. For instance, Gary Malkowski of Ontario, Canada was elected by parliament members to become a member of the provincial parliament (MPP) in Canada, and served for five years. I later helped campaign for deaf people such as Rodney Kunath, who ran for Ward 4 in Northampton, and for attorney Kelby Brick, who ran for city council in Greenbelt, Maryland. Unfortunately, neither won, but they helped bring awareness to deaf people's presence and skills. In the 1990s, Bruce White ran for and was elected to the City Council in College Park, Maryland, and Corinne Brennan-Dore won an election for the school board in Hadley, Massachusetts. It's always a good feeling to see other deaf people run for public office. I also worked with Mark Shriver in his run for Congress in 2002, and Kathleen Kennedy Townsend for Maryland Governor (President Kennedy's nephew and niece, respectively), and continued being active for numerous political causes. During this time period, Eunice Kennedy (President Kennedy's sister) and her husband Sargent Shriver threw Linda a surprise birthday party at their home in Potomac, Maryland.

Over the years, I've received a number of awards, and some of my most cherished ones include:

- Clarke School Alumni Association Hall of Fame
- RIT-NTID Distinguished Alumni Award
- Dean Junior College Distinguished Alumni Award
- Gallaudet University Alumni Association Laurent Clerc Cultural Fund Award
- National Association of the Deaf President's Award

Each and every award was earned because of the community's and my family's support, and the hard work we all did.

All Grown Up

All three of our children attended Clarke School for the Deaf. Kevin Jr. was four when he entered Clarke. He remained there for two years before he was mainstreamed at Jackson Street School. He went on to Smith Day School, Eaglebrook School, and then on to Suffield Academy. He didn't receive any support services at any of the schools he attended given that they were private schools and therefore not bound by the

ADA. It was challenging for him to be in a fully mainstreamed boarding school environment with no support except from his family. Kevin Jr. attended American University in Washington, DC, where he finally received interpreting services, and graduated with a bachelor's degree in criminal justice. He went on to get a master's degree in deaf education with an emphasis in special programs in deafness from Gallaudet University. Kevin Jr. has been fortunate to have worked for the U.S. Senate, the Massachusetts Department of Elementary and Secondary Education, and Boston Children's Hospital. He is married to Anna Larson, and they have a son, Kevin John Nolan III.

Kristi Ann first entered the Parent-Infant program at Clarke and stayed on until the age of 14, when she completed the curriculum. At her request, she attended the Model Secondary School for the Deaf (MSSD) in Washington, DC. While at MSSD, she was mainstreamed for part of the day at nearby private Gonzaga College High School. Upon graduation, she moved to California to attend California State University, Northridge (CSUN) before transferring to the University of California, Los Angeles (UCLA) and earning a bachelor's degree in history. She then received a master's degree in deaf education from CSUN. At the age of twenty-two, she became a self-contained classroom teacher at a public school in Los Angeles where she taught deaf children for six years. She then moved to Washington, DC, where she taught at Kendall Demonstration Elementary School for twelve years before becoming a stay-at-home mother to raise her two children, Jack and Rose, with her husband, Guang "Jax" Chuang.

Keith entered the Parent-Infant program at Clarke and remained there until he was 12 years old, when he was mainstreamed with support services at Wood Middle School in Rockville, Maryland. He then attended high school at the Maryland School for the Deaf and graduated. He went to CSUN where he received both bachelor's and master's degrees in political science and deaf education, respectively. He now teaches in the high school social studies department at the Maryland School for the Deaf and has established a cadet program at the school, passing on knowledge acquired from his ROTC days to new generations of deaf students who may one day serve our country as a member of our nation's armed forces. He married Gillian Lawrence in June 2019.

Life Today

After all the excitement of leaping over obstacles to victory, Linda and I now reside in Lake Worth, Florida. Throughout life, I have always loved being with people. Much of this outgoing attitude has always been within me, but was heightened by my being deaf. Despite the fact that I never really knew who my parents and siblings were aside from the superficial relationships I had with them, they never stopped me from pursuing my dreams. I also believe strongly that without the support I received from my wife Linda, our children, and my close friends, I would never have gotten this far. I continue to believe that deaf people can succeed at whatever goals and objectives they set for themselves. It is crucial to provide encouragement to people to push the limits of what is considered possible for deaf people. Sometimes that little nudge or encouragement is all it takes.

Everyone is different, but perhaps no one said it better than my father when he was interviewed by the local Attleboro newspaper, the Sun Chronicle, about me:

"In this world, as they say, everyone moves to the beat of a different drummer and though some hear the beat while others cannot, everyone must step to the rhythm. And those who work at it themselves, like Kevin, will gain most."

The Nolan family in Summer 2017: (front) Me and Linda; (Back, L-R) Kevin Jr., Anna, Kevin III, Jax, Jack, Kristi Ann (pregnant with Rose), and Keith.

69133170R00080

Made in the USA
Columbia, SC
18 August 2019